Dealing with Dementia

My Journey as Caregiver for My Husband

By Joanne Hand

Dealing with Dementia — My Journey as Caregiver for My Husband
Copyright © 2023 by Joanne Hand

All rights reserved. No part of this book may be used or reproduced in any manner whatsoever without written permission except in the case of brief quotations in critical articles or reviews.

Cover design by Joy Nicholson

Bible verses quoted are cited, per chapter, in the Endnotes.

Unless otherwise indicated, all Scripture quotations are taken from the Holy Bible, New Living Translation, copyright © 1996, 2004, 2007. Used by permission of Tyndale House Publishers Inc., Carol Stream, Illinois 60188. All rights reserved.

Scripture quotations marked ESV are from the Holy Bible, English Standard Version, copyright © 2001, 2007, 2011, 2016 by Crossway Bibles, a division of Good News Publishers. Used by permission. All rights reserved.

Scripture quotations marked NKJV are taken from the New King James Version®. NKJV® Copyright © 1982 by Thomas Nelson. Used by permission. All rights reserved.

Verses marked NIV are taken from The Holy Bible, New International Version® NIV® Copyright © 1973, 1978, 1984, 2011 by Biblica, Inc. Used by permission of Zondervan. All rights reserved worldwide. www.zondervan.com The "NIV" and "New International Version" are trademarks registered in the United States Patent and Trademark Office by Biblica, Inc.™

Scripture quotations marked KJV are taken from the King James Version, 1611, 1769, public domain.

Scripture quotations marked (CEV) are from the Contemporary English Version Copyright © 1991, 1992, 1995 by American Bible Society, Used by Permission.

Scripture quotations marked AMP are taken from the Amplified® Bible (AMP), Copyright © 2015 by The Lockman Foundation. Used by permission. www.lockman.org

All praise to God, the Father of our
Lord Jesus Christ. God is our merciful Father
and the source of all comfort. He comforts us
in all our troubles so that we can comfort others.
When they are troubled, we will be able to
give them the same comfort God has given us.

2 Corinthians 1:3-4 (NLT)

About the Author

At 84 years of age, Joanne Hand is publishing her first book. Joanne dearly loved and served as the primary caregiver for her husband Babby, who was diagnosed with vascular dementia. After several years, Babby succumbed to complications from dementia and passed away in 2009.

Born in Michigan, Joanne moved to Pelham, Georgia with Babby in 1962 and became an active resident for nearly sixty years. Without the love and support of the great citizens of Mitchell County, Georgia, Joanne could not have succeeded in her journey as a caregiver. A multitude of friends, colleagues from work, members from her local church, downtown shop owners, city officials and especially doctors and nurses all took a personal interest in Joanne and Babby during the difficult years of dementia.

From 1981 until 2001, Joanne was a news writer and editorial columnist for the *Pelham Journal* — a weekly hometown newspaper. She officially retired from her journalist career in 2001, but continued to contribute editorials to the *Journal* through 2013.

Joanne has two sons, two daughters-in-law and three grandchildren. She currently lives in Florida.

Acknowledgements

I can't thank the following people enough for assisting me in the many phases of editing to help see this book to completion:

    Ken Chivers
    Ben Gunter
    Addison Hand
    Avery Hand
    David & Shannon Hand
    Beth Kuligowski
    Bob & Kathy Mac Leod
    Maxine McDonald
    Dan & Diane Peters
    Joey Womble

A special thank you to Joy Nicholson for a beautiful cover design.

    I also owe a debt of gratitude to the wonderful people of Pelham, Georgia who have shown much kindness to me over the years. Without their love and support, I could not have sustained my journey as a caregiver for my husband. There are far too many people to list who helped lift me up and provided help in amazing ways. It is said that

Pelham is a special place because of its people. If you have ever called Pelham your home, my heart is with you and I am grateful for you!

Contents

About the Author
Acknowledgements
Foreword i
Introduction ix

1. Lord, Help Us! 1
2. Getting to the Doctor 13
3. "On Eagle's Wings" 27
4. Therapy Lifelines 35
5. Dangerous Driving 43
6. Finding Comfort in a Grocery Store 47
7. Gift of Hope 57
8. His Name Is Fear 63
9. Worry Wrestling 69
10. Abundant Reassurance 75
11. People-Angels 85
12. More People-Angels 95
13. Nearing the End 101
14. God's Grace in Dementia 107

15. Falling in Love with a Pilot 115
16. Wrestling Through the 23rd Psalm 123
17. A Temporary Reprieve 129
18. Peace in the Final Days 139
19. Alligator Goodbye 145
20. The Musical Ice Cream Truck 151
21. Comfort from Heaven 157
22. A Gift from Babby 161

Afterword 167
Appendix 171
Endnotes 203

Foreword
Written by David Hand

Joanne Hand, my mother, wrote this book; it has been my privilege to serve as her assistant editor. The following are my introductory comments on the amazing true story my mom has written:

My dad was a man of few words. Mom has always been more of a conversationalist. They were quite different in personality. He enjoyed witty, dry humor. She has never been known as a lighthearted laugh box. Dad tended to grasp the big picture of present events in context of the past. Mom has usually focused on the present, taking things at face value. They often had differing opinions but found a way to link arms, move forward and enjoy each other's deep friendship and sweet companionship.

My dad's name was Larrabee Davenport Hand, Jr. He was born in southwest Georgia during the early 1930s. In the deep south, it wasn't uncommon for the firstborn son in the family to be named after his father and for his full name to be a slow drawl of a mouthful. Dad had three sisters who, reportedly, during their childhood could never easily pronounce "Larrabee" so they called him "Babby" (BAB-bee) instead. It stuck. That was the name most folks called him.

Dad grew up in a rural, agriculture-centric town amidst an extended family with several of his cousins intertwined in his daily life. He was witty. Lighthearted. Caring. Not slow to come to help or show concern. He was very reserved in his speech, introverted and somewhat stoic but always a faithful friend. After earning a degree in chemical engineering, he served briefly as an officer in the Air Force and then was hired by the Tennessee Valley Authority in northwest Alabama. There he met my mom, got married and brought her back to his hometown of Pelham, Georgia to work in a family-owned business. They lived there and enjoyed a great life for the next forty-five years.

Then dementia set in. It felt sudden. "What's dementia? Does he really have THAT?" I asked. As I quickly learned, there are many types of dementia. Until the last few decades, medical science has understood little and had thin answers. In oversimplified terms, the effects of dementia make the brain forget how to make connections with memories and physical capabilities.

We all, at one time or another, struggle on some level with short term forgetfulness. As the brain grows older it slows down. Without an ability to remember and make connections to people, memories, capabilities and knowledge, we can feel hopeless and deeply limited. It is maddening to watch a loved one experience a drastic form of forgetfulness such as dementia.

From my personal observations of people who have dementia, it appears that no two dementia patients progress or worsen at the same rate with the disease. Symptoms often have common threads, but from one patient to the next, how each one struggles with the disease can look different. For my dad, noticeable changes in his short term memory and cognitive abilities appeared several months before he reached seventy years of age. Since he never was very talkative, discerning how much of his vocabulary or verbal capacity was whittled away by dementia at any specific point in time was challenging. But eventually, about four years after the onset of vascular dementia, he could not string enough words together to speak an intelligible sentence. His ability to understand words spoken to him declined, but not as sharply as his ability to speak. It was obvious that he could understand — even towards the end. A couple of short words or a smile or nod was how he marginally stayed engaged in a conversation. Sadly, during the last few months of his life, he couldn't recognize his friends and some of his loved ones. Almost all of his memories were gone. His ability to walk ceased. Other physical capabilities ground to a halt. He died at age seventy-four.

My mom did an excellent job caring for Dad. She believed that as long as Dad could walk and have sufficient cognitive abilities, it was best to care for him at home. It wasn't her desire to send him to a care facility, although she knew that might be a possibility one day and was mentally prepared for it. For the last several months of his life, Mom dealt with "the new normal" of Dad's declining cognitive abilities — which were redefined and reset by dementia almost on a weekly basis. She often grew anxious. She became exhausted. She slowly lost conversational connection with the man who faithfully cared for her and would listen to her cares. It was heart-wrenching. Yet in the midst of it all, God provided love and hope.

As I watched my dad grow mentally and physically less able from dementia and my mom grow more exhausted and anxious from caring for him, I grappled with why this was happening. Sometimes it felt hopeless. God never withdrew His presence or care for my dad during those days, but it felt like Dad was trapped in a dark room with only one exit door — a locked door — and God wasn't providing the key to escape. In the Bible there is a story recorded of a man who was born blind, whom Jesus healed when the man was well into his adult years. Jesus' disciples asked, "Who sinned? This man or his parents, that he was born blind?" The parents of the blind man were caregivers. They constantly had to watch out for their blind son, protecting him and providing for him in ways he couldn't provide for himself. I'd be willing to bet that both he and his parents felt hopeless at times.

    Long ago, people often thought that physical disabilities or severe illnesses were a result of your own evildoing. Thus, Jesus' disciples asked their Master who was responsible for this terrible judgment upon the blind man and his family. Jesus' response tells us a lot about the central core truth of how God shows kindness to people in a broken world. This central truth is called the gospel, or "good news." It is my desire and my mom's ultimate hope that you will understand how this gospel is truly the story beneath the story of how my dad struggled with dementia and how she was able to care for him.

DEALING WITH DEMENTIA

Dementia is all about the curse of forgetting and being forgotten. The gospel is about God remembering. Even if you have believed in God for all of your life, dealing with dementia brings up a lot of very hard questions:

> Why does dementia exist?
> What does God think about dementia?
> Will God forsake or forget people with dementia?
> How do I care for myself as I care for my loved one who has dementia?

In the appendix of this book, I have attempted to write partial answers to some of these complex questions. Some answers are just a starting point, but I hope they will help.

I've also explained the story of the blind man a bit further in the appendix. Hopefully you'll be encouraged to read how the gospel redeems and reverses the curse of dementia and the much greater curse of sin that affects every human. I have included a couple of brief details of how my dad came to know and experience God in a distinct, personal way through the gospel. During his mid-fifties, my father's life was deeply changed by God and many people noticed. To write the complete story of his transformation and the people he touched would mean writing another book.

Dad's death was expected yet somewhat sudden. In the years following, Mom found that writing about her experiences as a caregiver was extremely cathartic.

Most of the chapters of this book were written by my mom before Dad died. Although they have been edited more recently, some chapters were individually published as editorial articles in the newspaper during the last year and months before Dad went to heaven. It was providential that Mom wrote the details as they unfolded. Today — some twelve to eighteen years after the events happened — many of the conversations, details and specific encounters have completely faded from Mom's mind. She too has begun to experience a slowness of mind and words, although on a different level and intensity. However, because of her written record — many journal entries, several newspaper articles and notes, emails and letters to friends — she gratefully drew from these sources to coalesce the pieces of the story into a book.

This book is her story, from her point of view, of how God made the dementia journey a walk of hope, redemption and love.

DEALING WITH DEMENTIA

Babby & Joanne Hand, December 2005

Introduction

I could hardly believe what I was hearing. A national television newscaster I respect was interviewing a physician about Alzheimer's disease. They came to the conclusion that nothing really helps people with Alzheimer's disease, even in the early stages. I wanted to shout at them, "That's not true!" At least that wasn't true for my husband who struggled with another form of dementia.

Yes, I know there is no cure for Alzheimer's, or for any kind of dementia. However, as the home caregiver for my husband who suffered from vascular dementia, I know many things that helped him (and me) when his sharp mind became more and more muddled.

True, our dementia journey was a heartbreaking struggle that lasted about six years. Watching him gradually lose his cognitive abilities, his memories, and his judgment regarding driving and financial matters was scary and heartbreaking. But I thank God that his struggles and confusion were interspersed with gracious help from people in our small town. For instance, my husband enjoyed walking for exercise, but after dementia began fogging up his mind, sometimes he got lost wandering in neighborhoods many blocks away from our home. I'm deeply thankful that at those times someone noticed him, recognized who he was, and called me, letting me know where I could come get him and take him home.

Many people knew about our situation and cared enough to tell me they were praying for us. I believe their prayers as well as mine helped us more than anything. Sometimes I could see surprising answers to prayers that helped my husband, and other times I could feel God using people's prayers to sustain my strength, and give me a peace that passes understanding.

Also I thank God that even in the upsetting times, my husband sometimes surprised me by hugging me and telling me he loved me far more often than he ever did before. Hugs from friends also helped. Even cards from friends and acquaintances saying they were thinking of us lifted my spirits.

Initially I wrote about our situation in the editorial page of our hometown weekly newspaper, *The Pelham Journal*, where I had been a columnist and reporter for 20 years until I retired in 2001.

These narrative articles told the various ways I believed God was helping us deal with this mind-stealing disease.

Each editorial column I wrote included my photo. It's common for newspapers to include a small, square crop of the author's face. This helped people recognize me when they saw me in public places such as the grocery store. This also created opportunities for conversations about my husband's dementia.

The positive feedback I received from readers was gratifying. People called me on the phone, emailed me, or talked to me wherever they saw me out in the community. They all thanked me for writing about our situation because dementia touches many families, but people don't usually talk about it, especially if it's in their own family.

Writing about our situation helped me deal with the stress. Even better, it gave me an opportunity to tell what eased our way through the hard times, showing readers what might help them deal with their own difficulties. Looking back, I can see that our dementia journey was a faith journey. Even though my husband's mind failed, God never failed us. How? That's what this story is all about. In His timing, and in His ways, God always answered my many desperate prayers for help. Also, the Lord comforted me when I needed comfort the most, as only God could do, way beyond what I could imagine. That's not to say I always received answers the way I asked, or when I asked. But now I see how God helped us through the heartbreaking downward spiral of dementia, in spite of my worries and fears.

In order to jog my memory about specific details for this book, I have drawn from the newspaper editorial columns I wrote, emails I sent or received concerning our situation, and entries from my prayer journal to tell our story about how we dealt with dementia. I'm grateful for these personal records. Without them I wouldn't have a coherent story to tell, only a mishmash jumble of memories. I don't trust my memories without the backup of these records to trace and tell the progression of our story. My hope is that this book will help readers deal with their own difficulties from some of the lessons I've learned.

1
Lord, Help Us!

What could be wrong? I asked myself with growing apprehension. *Why is Babby driving so recklessly on this busy interstate?* Babby, a nickname which family and friends called my husband whose given name was Larrabee, always had been a safe driver. He never drove over the speed limit, and he always maintained safe distances behind other cars and trucks. *Why is he driving so dangerously now? This is totally unlike him*, I thought, my heart racing, my hands clenching nervously. We were driving on Georgia Interstate 75 on our way to visit our son David and his family at their home near Atlanta.

DEALING WITH DEMENTIA

That October day the trees blazed in joyful colors, but I hardly noticed. Cars and semi-trucks whizzed and wove through fast-moving traffic on all sides. Babby tried to keep up, zooming close behind a mammoth truck rumbling much faster than the speed limit, and then briefly straddled erratically between two lanes. Suddenly Babby began looking for ways to pass the speeding truck! *"Lord, help us!"* I prayed silently.

To my relief the semi-truck zoomed around another car, leaving us in its wake, while traffic opened up and slowed down to a sane speed. Babby quickly shifted lanes, heading toward the right outside lane. But I knew we had a left exit off the interstate coming up in a couple of miles. *What is he doing?*

"I've got to pull over and stop," he said. A rest stop loomed to the right, and he safely negotiated the turn, parking under a shade tree. "I'm lost," he admitted. "I don't remember how to get to David's house. Will you call him and ask him to come get us?" I was shocked, but thankful, and puzzled too.

We had driven to our son's house a few times previously, and I thought he knew the way well, even with the tricky turnoffs. Whenever we went anywhere together, he always drove, which suited me fine because he was such a safe driver. But he seemed exhausted and confused now. I silently thanked God that he realized he needed help, and asked for it, which must have been a hard thing for him to do.

Also I thanked God for the rest stop Babby spotted right when we needed it. Picking up the phone, I prayed that David would be at home, and breathed a sigh of relief when he answered, saying it would take him about a half hour to come meet us at the rest stop.

While we waited, Babby restlessly roamed around the parking lot. I staked out a spot near the entrance where I could see David drive in, and also see where our Ford Escort was parked. As I tried to relax, I told my racing heart to slow down so I could think straight. I took deep breaths.

What could be wrong? I asked myself over and over. I didn't even want to consider if Babby could be in the early stages of Alzheimer's disease, yet the thought intruded. True, his mother had Alzheimer's disease, and although his father was never diagnosed with dementia, in his elderly years he asked the same questions repeatedly, and would tell the same story of previous experiences over and over.

Babby didn't show any of the symptoms they showed, as far as I could tell. Nevertheless, it's in the family. *Could Babby's former employer be right?* I wondered. A few months earlier his employer had called me. "I need to tell you that Babby is headed home now. He just quit his job. Stormed into my office and said, 'I quit!' as he threw down his keys on my desk. I've never seen him angry like that. Something is wrong. You had better get him to a doctor," she said.

Babby exploded in anger? I wondered. He hardly ever got angry, much less exploded. However, he had confided to me several times in the previous months that he was struggling to keep up with the work his employer was piling on him, or at least that was his perception of the situation. He was the company's bookkeeper, a job well suited to his mathematical skills. His mind worked like a computer when it came to numbers and balancing books. He worked hard, always wanting to get a job done right, and on time. For the last several months he had worked late on weeknights as well as on weekends just to keep up with the job. Babby always saw his work through to completion. Thinking his boss was giving him more responsibilities than were reasonable, I seethed with anger. To make matters worse, his employer also told me he was making mistakes in his bookkeeping work. *Babby was making mistakes when it came to numbers?* That was most unusual. But surely that was because he was under so much stress trying to get everything done, I reasoned. I was glad he quit. He needed to retire, and he was plenty old enough at 69. We had retirement savings, and thanks to Babby's long-term planning, we could make it financially. Now that he was out from under the stress of his job, his mind could recover its clarity, I reasoned.

But what if it's more than stress? Casting about in my mind while we waited in the parking lot for our son to come guide us to his house, I tried to find some clues in Babby's recent behavior. I remembered that the day after Babby quit his job, we took a long-planned vacation sight-seeing in Savannah, followed by staying several days at Epworth by the Sea, a peaceful Methodist retreat center sheltered beneath towering live oak trees draped in Spanish moss on the eastern coast of Georgia.

On the first leg of our vacation, Babby didn't have any problems driving five hours from our home in Pelham to Savannah where we had never visited before. He had no problems driving to various locations within the historic city, and no trouble driving us from Savannah to the retreat center.

During our days at Epworth, we gathered with other people for worship, singing praise songs and familiar hymns. Joy filled my heart to overflowing, especially when I saw Babby smiling and clapping along with everyone else. The exuberant songs lifted us up, giving me the feeling that God was hugging us, and reassuring me. *Surely this must be a sign that Babby will be able to enjoy the retirement he deserves*, I thought.

Reinforcing my assessment, I remembered that he also didn't have any problems driving us back home after our vacation time at Epworth, and I didn't see any signs of mental difficulties once we got home. He did have some trouble remembering names, but don't most people when they get older?

At home, Babby settled into an easy-going daily routine. Every morning except Sunday he walked three blocks from our house to a local diner called Tank & Tummy for breakfast, eating and talking with several retired men who always invited him to join them at their table. After breakfast he would walk by the downtown shops and then sometimes ramble across the single set of railroad tracks running north-south through the middle of town, to take a loop around the neighborhood where he grew up. Babby was born and raised in Pelham. Everything in town was familiar to him.

As a boy prior to World War II, he saw electric street lights installed in the downtown area and a traffic signal set up at the main four-way intersection of two dusty roads and one state highway. The town became modern and the population slowly grew, yet the people and pace of life never seemed to rush. As he strolled, Babby noticed that several streets, shops and a few neighborhoods remained mostly unchanged from the days when he was a young man. He walked partly for exercise, and partly just to see what was going on around town. Our normal weekly routines included attending Sunday School and church on Sunday mornings at our local United Methodist Church, just two short blocks away from our house. In addition, Babby volunteered regularly with a local prison ministry. Life was good then, especially since I was retired too.

But now waiting in the parking lot for our son to arrive and take us to his home, I wondered, *What's next? How will we get back to our home in South Georgia after our visit, especially if Babby won't let me drive?* The thought of his driving us several hundred miles home the reckless way he had been driving on the busy interstate filled me with dread.

Finally David and his wife Shannon drove into the parking lot. After exchanging welcoming hugs with everyone, David drove his dad in our car, and I rode with Shannon to their house.

We had a lovely fall visit, especially with our grandkids, two girls and a boy — ages six, three, and one at the time. They adored their Pops, as they called Babby, and he couldn't stop smiling every time he looked at them. He enjoyed reading to them from their story books, his arms curled around them as they snuggled close to him on the couch.

Since we were visiting with them in October, the month he was born, we celebrated his 70th birthday with a chocolate birthday cake which Shannon made and decorated with white frosting scalloped around the top and bottom edges. Candles on top were lit as the children gathered around him sitting at the head of the dining room table. The children excitedly helped him blow out those candles as we all sang, "Happy Birthday" amid laughter and giggles and picture taking.

All too soon it was time for us to return home to South Georgia. That morning I offered to drive us, but Babby refused. Then I reminded him that there was a better way to go back home than high-speed Interstate 75. That better way was a two-lane highway we'd driven many times previously, called Old Highway 19. It was a slower route, but safer and more scenic. I urged Babby to head that way, but he indicated he was determined to get on the busy interstate. All I could do was pray.

Driving down the main road from our son's house, he spotted an exit that he thought would take us to the interstate. The exit led up a steep incline, and at the top, a sign pointed south to Highway 19. "Look, Babby!" I exclaimed. "That's old U.S. 19! That will take us straight home!" He turned north, instead of south, but soon realized he was going in the wrong direction, and turned around and went south on old U.S. 19, a scenic two-lane highway. *Thank heavens we are going in the right direction, and the traffic is light.* We came to a small town where there was a sign pointing to I-75. I revved up my silent prayers. *Please, Lord, keep him driving on Highway 19, and not turn to the busy interstate where he drove so dangerously before!* I think he saw the sign to the interstate, but his brain could not react quickly enough to make the turn at that exit. *Thank You, Lord! Thank you!* I breathed, when he kept driving on Highway 19. That's the way it was all the way home. Every time we came to a town where there was a sign pointing to I-75, Babby drove past the exit turn in spite of his intentions of getting on the interstate. At the slower speeds and with light traffic, his driving was safe, yet it seemed to greatly tax him.

Apparently he didn't realize how dangerously he drove on I-75 with the big trucks and fast, crazy traffic. Driving in traffic was never a problem with him before. But it was a big problem now. Obviously his judgment had become impaired, I realized. His brain wasn't working clearly.

I've never prayed so hard, asking God to keep us on the safe road, then thanking God every time we went past the turnoff to the fast traveling I-75. The two-lane route on Old Highway 19 meandered through small towns and farmlands with green pastures. By the time we got home, I felt like kissing the ground. Instead, I silently thanked God. Yet I sensed something was wrong with Babby's mental faculties. *Isn't he too young to have dementia?* I wondered. His sharpness had diminished, I realized, and his behavior was erratic, such as when he snapped at his employer, and drove recklessly which was unlike him. Something was wrong with his brain, I concluded. I knew it wasn't stress, and I couldn't explain it away any longer.

"He needs to see a doctor," I told the Lord in my prayer journal after I collected my wits at home. *"But I can't force him. Love is patient, not forceful."* I decided to wait and see. *"Surely You will show us the right way. Hold my hand, Lord; hold both our hands, please!"*

Babby (known as "Pops" by our grandkids) at his 70th birthday party

2

Getting to the Doctor

Life at home bumped along for a while as I prayed for clarity of mind for Babby and guidance for us both. Over and over I asked myself and God, *When and how should I bring up his need to see a doctor?* I hate waiting on answers. Knots of what ifs tangled up my mind and sometimes my stomach. *I must try to relax and trust God to work it out*, I told myself. *Help me, Lord!* Then I remembered what Jesus told his frightened disciples as quoted in John's gospel, the 14th chapter:

"Peace I leave with you; my peace I give you. I do not give to you as the world gives. Do not let your hearts be troubled and do not be afraid."[1]

Those words played over and over in my mind. To my surprise, the promise of His peace did indeed fill me, a strong peace that steadied me. I knew I might lose that sense of peace from time to time, but I told myself that I could always ask Jesus to provide His promised peace as many times as I needed.

Songs also helped me. For instance, right in the middle of uncertain times at home, each Sunday for a whole month at church we sang the same Easter resurrection song called "Because He Lives,"[2] by Bill and Gloria Gaither. Referring to Jesus Christ, the words of that refrain reassured me. Jesus is always with me through His Holy Spirit, helping me no matter what happens, working all things for good.

I needed that song in my heart to shield me from Babby's sudden, dementia-driven, angry eruptions at home when he said snarling things I knew he didn't mean, then stormed out of the house. That's when I fell to my knees, desperately asking the Lord to fill Babby's heart to overflowing with God's love once again.

Many years earlier both of us had attended a spiritual retreat called "Walk to Emmaus" based on the gospel writer Luke's account of the risen Christ appearing to travelers on the road to Emmaus in Luke 24:13-35. Before I attended that retreat, I had known intellectually that God loves me. However, I had never been touched by the wonder and joy of God's loving, guiding presence until I attended that retreat. That experience filled my heart with refreshing newness of life providing ongoing peace and comfort. Babby seemed to be affected in a similar way, too, which drew us closer together.

Remembering that retreat, I felt confident that God could refill Babby's heart with His love to overflowing continually. I just needed to keep praying for that.

One day after Babby slung hurtful words at me again, then angrily left the house, I grabbed the leash for our small dog Chance, and took a walk in our neighborhood park. Gulping back tears, I silently told God that with His help, with *lots* of His supernatural help, I could bear, at least to a certain extent, watching Babby lose his mind bit by bit. *But please, please hear me, Lord, I cannot bear to lose his love!* The thought of losing Babby's love literally hurt my heart as I cried out to God while I slowly walked Chance along the tree-lined sidewalk. Watching Chance try to chase some teasing squirrels while he tugged on his leash yipping eagerly was just the comic relief I needed to make me laugh. Then we headed home as I thanked God for that amusing spirit lifter, while also thanking Him for Chance, for towering shade trees in the park, and even for silly squirrels.

Not long after Chance and I returned home, Babby quietly came back home too. "Can you forgive me?" he asked, touching my shoulder. We clung to each other in a big hug. "Oh yes," I said, adding, "I love you." I was dumbfounded that he even remembered his hostile eruption, and I was deeply grateful he asked for forgiveness, which I gladly granted.

Gradually, over time, these angry, hurtful episodes decreased, and his affectionate, kind ways increased! I could hardly believe it! Before the disease took over, Babby and I had what I considered a good marriage. I like to talk, and Babby was more the silent type who mostly listened, but we did talk together about things that were important to us. As friends noted, Babby didn't talk much, but when he did say something, he made a lot of sense. We had walked through conflict and some disagreements before, but always talked everything through to the good.

Babby was helpful about doing household tasks such as loading and unloading the dishwasher, taking out the garbage and trash, vacuuming the carpets and doing small repairs around the house. He enjoyed mowing our lawn once a week using a non-motorized, antique lawn mower, saying it gave him good exercise. He cooked our meals when I was sick, although that was not his favorite activity. When our two sons were elementary school age, he always cooked breakfast for them. We shared a love of dogs and cats, usually having one of each as pets. And he was always good about remembering my birthday with a night out at a restaurant. Also we celebrated our wedding anniversary in June, usually by spending a week at Jekyll Island off the coast of Georgia. On Valentine's Day he never failed to give me a card inscribed with sweet sentiments and a box of chocolates.

    Wherever we walked together downtown, or even to church — just two blocks away from our house — we usually held hands. One Sunday morning as our Sunday School class got underway, someone asked Babby what he had been doing during the previous week. "Oh, whatever she tells me to do," he quipped immediately, nodding at me and grinning with his wacky sense of humor. Although he was joking, what he said was true, and I was grateful for his helpfulness in all manner of things. His droll sense of humor salted our entire fifty years of marriage, always making me smile or laugh. I was grateful I could still catch glimpses of his quick, witty sense of humor.

Even after dementia first set in, Babby always opened up our church doors first thing every Sunday morning, and locked up after the services. This was one of many ways he enjoyed serving quietly and behind the scenes. During the worship service he joined in singing the hymns. Even though he couldn't sing in tune, I was proud of him for singing! It didn't matter to me that he couldn't carry a tune, singing in a kind of monotone as he pronounced the words. After all, the lyrics carry the message of the hymns. Singing the right notes is good, our choir director often told the choir members, but it's the message of the hymns that's most important. Babby's singing touched my heart and made me love him all the more. I imagine it pleased God too, because Psalm 98:4 says, "Make a joyful noise unto the Lord, all the earth..."[3] It doesn't say anything about singing in tune!

While I was grateful for these and many other habits that drew us close together in our marriage, we didn't hug frequently, or verbally express our love for each other very often. But after dementia set in, that changed, much to my astonishment! Two or three times a day he spontaneously hugged me and told me he loved me. It was delightful! I couldn't thank God enough! Apparently God was answering my frantic prayers, refilling Babby's heart to the brim and running over with sweet affection. That is the only way I can explain it. His mind was still foggy and forgetful, but I was comforted by his hugs and words of love. I enjoyed it while it lasted, knowing that as the disease progressed, unpredictable episodes of anger could explode again from time to time. That was all the more reason why I needed to get him to a doctor before things got worse. But how, especially if he didn't see the need?

While I was trying to figure out how I could convince him to see a doctor, I began having some temporary and puzzling symptoms of my own. Sporadically for a couple of weeks, I had trouble sleeping at night. I could feel my heart thumping in my chest — which seemed to be at an erratic pace. I felt no pain or tightness in my chest, but the feeling of the increasingly heavy pounding would wake me up. Thump, thump, ka-thump! *What in the world was going on?* Usually I could go back to sleep after some time. It was concerning, but not painful. However, on one such occasion I was awake all night, and it felt like my heart would beat out of my chest. I called my family doctor, and after I explained to her what I was experiencing, she told me she would see me that same morning. I asked Babby to drive me there. By this time my heart was settling down, and I felt fine. Although my doctor ruled out the possibility that I was having a heart attack, she referred me to a heart specialist in a nearby town to get additional tests.

When we got home, Babby showed me a pamphlet he had picked up at the doctor's office that listed some of the common symptoms of Alzheimer's disease. I could hardly believe it. *He noticed it? He read it? And he brought it home for me to read?* This caught me by surprise and waved a little flag of hope. "Why don't we sit down at the kitchen table and go over it," I suggested, and we did. Handing me the pamphlet, Babby said the symptoms sounded familiar, meaning he recognized them in himself. Calmly, but with an undercurrent of concern, Babby began telling me how he felt about this. He indicated that he was puzzled and troubled when confusion overtook him sometimes, and he couldn't find words that stubbornly stayed hidden in his mind. He sometimes forgot even family names, and working on the computer at home became too difficult for him, he admitted.

"But look, Babby," I said. "This pamphlet says medication can help in the early stage. Would you be willing to see our local doctor?" Much to my relief, he said that sounded like a good idea. The waiting had paid off! I breathed a prayer of thanksgiving for an answer to prayer. Then I made an appointment for us to see Babby's doctor about his symptoms.

When I saw the cardiologist a month or so later about my heart, extensive tests showed nothing wrong! I was grateful that my temporary symptoms served the purpose of getting Babby to our family doctor through the pamphlet Babby found at the office.

When we saw Babby's doctor, tests ruled out several possibilities that might be causing Babby's symptoms. After that, the doctor asked him a series of simple questions. "Who is the current President of our country? What state do we live in? What season are we in? What is today's date?" Many of these questions Babby couldn't answer correctly, although he sailed through a few other basic questions without any hesitation. After weighing the results of all the tests, the doctor said he thought Babby was in the early stage of some kind of dementia, although he was not sure which kind. As the doctor explained, Alzheimer's disease is just one form of dementia. The doctor prescribed a well known medication for dementia, saying that it should probably help, at least for a while.

Listening to the prognosis, I had mixed emotions. I was thankful he was getting treatment, and he was now under the care of a doctor. I liked his doctor. He treated Babby like he would his own father, as he told us. But the situation was sobering nonetheless. My heart ached for Babby.

As for Babby, at that time I'm not sure he understood the meaning of the word dementia. He didn't ask any questions. He just seemed to put it behind him and accepted whatever came next.

Babby didn't usually get hung up with anxious thoughts or worry about things like I did. I did enough worrying for both of us. Worry short circuits trust in God. Anxious thoughts are natural sometimes, but I learned then that I needed to ask for the peace that Jesus gives. As I discovered, His peace can lead to trusting God's guidance and reassurance, remembering His constant, caring presence.

Regardless, I made one determined decision: I would not keep his diagnosis a secret. I wanted people to know about our situation so they could pray for Babby, and for me. I knew we couldn't make this journey alone. We were going to need lots of prayer, and lots of help. That's why I wanted to write about our dementia journey in our local newspaper. I figured that would generate more prayers from readers, and it would give me a way to share what helped us both along the way, including answered prayers.

Some people asked me what Babby thought of my writing about him. When I first started writing the series, I showed him what I had written, and asked him how he felt about it. I can't remember what he said in response, but it didn't seem to bother him. I thanked God for that, because I thought sharing our story would be an encouragement for readers. Yes, his condition was difficult for me, as well as heartbreaking, and a heavy burden to carry. I don't want to minimize that. But from time to time something always lightened the load and renewed my strength. Only God could have done that, I believe.

Nevertheless, I worried about the struggles we would face. *How would God help us with the mountains of difficulties on this journey through dementia?* I worried about how I would even know how to pray.

One time when I was sick with a fever, I deeply wanted to pray but I was so miserable and weak that I didn't feel up to praying out loud. Babby was a man of few words naturally, well before his dementia began stealing words from his brain. However, many months after dementia set in, he struggled to string even a few words intelligibly together for a simple sentence. Nevertheless, on impulse I asked Babby to pray for me. He didn't ask any questions. He simply wrapped his arms around me and began praying with compassion, asking our Lord to help me and heal me. To my amazement, his prayer was beautifully articulate, words pouring out through him with supportive strength and comfort like I had never heard before. A sense of peace washed over me. I knew without a doubt that the Holy Spirit had prayed through him, blessing us both with reassurance. "Thank you, Lord, thank you, Babby," I said softly in response.

During another time of distress, God responded to my prayerful plea for help in such an amazing way I hesitate to write about it. *Was this experience the result of my overactive imagination?* Even though it was totally unexpected, I know it was real and I never could have dreamed this up. This experience happened during one of those times when Babby exploded in anger, hurling hurtful, hateful words at me, then stomped out the door. I knew the dementia caused those hateful words to erupt, not Babby in his right mind, or from his heart. But still, the words hurt deeply. I sank to my knees in front of my chair at my desk. *Oh Lord, restore Babby's love, please!* I pleaded. *Fill his heart to overflowing with your loving kindness, Lord, the way you've done before. Help me, and help Babby! He doesn't know what he's saying.*

While I was crying out to God, sometimes in halting words, sometimes silently in my mind, I felt a gentle hand on my shoulder which extended to my other shoulder in a tender embrace. I looked up, thinking Babby had come back and was trying to comfort me. But no one was there. No one I could see, anyway. I was taken aback and tried to recalibrate my sensory system. My crying and emotions had shaken me physically. Yet the reassuring embrace – like a gentle hug from strong hands – felt completely real. Did God send an unseen angel to comfort me? I don't know. All I know is I'm filled with grateful awe when I think of that experience. I believe this comfort was given to me as a witness to God's amazing grace in times of trouble. Although it never has happened again, it has remained a touchstone of comforting reassurance – the reassurance of God's caring, constant presence.

3
"On Eagle's Wings"

"Look at all those people!" I whispered to a fellow choir member one Sunday night in December. "The church is filled!" Several times during the week leading up to this program I had asked God to send a multitude to our Christmas worship service, but this was more than I dared expect.

But where was my husband? He wasn't in his usual seat and I couldn't spot him. Less than a week earlier he had started taking medication for dementia. Sometimes he got confused. Perhaps he walked back home. Or maybe he decided not to come even though he told me he would walk to the church after I went early for our afternoon choir rehearsal before the Christmas program.

I started praying silently, putting him in God's hands. Then I put my heart into singing the Christmas music, some carols familiar and warming, some relatively new to me and filled with wonder. The joyful music swept away my worry. Until, that is, one of our choir members, a soprano soloist, began singing "On Eagle's Wings"[1] by Michael Joncas, based on Psalm 91. Babby loved that song as much as I do. I started scanning the congregation once again, praying that he could hear this soaring song.

That's when I noticed my husband sitting in the back shadows of the church. I smiled in thankful relief as the soloist sang the lifting chorus. The lyrics brought to mind Psalm 91:

"Those who live in the shelter of the Most High will find rest in the shadow of the Almighty. This I declare about the LORD: He alone is my refuge, my place of safety; he is my God, and I trust him."[2]

Our Lord never leaves me alone in my fears. He teaches me to trust Him to be my Helper and lifts me above my fears. He holds me close to Him throughout whatever fearful difficulties I may face, even my husband's dementia.

It was like God sang this song straight into my heart, reassuring me that He will always hold Babby in the palm of His hands no matter what, and He will always raise me up on the wings of His upholding presence. I tended to forget this sometimes, especially when I felt alone, grounded in worry and grief. But God has a way of reminding me that He is with us always, despite my feelings to the contrary. Furthermore, He sometimes gave me gifts of joy to reinforce that reminder. For instance, every morning right after Babby left our house and walked a few blocks to Tank and Tummy for breakfast, I also would take a walk to focus on the beautiful things God had made. Breathing deeply as I walked through our tree-lined neighborhood, I felt invigorated looking and listening for something lovely that would lift my spirits. Sometimes God's gift was a mockingbird singing its joyful songs or a squirrel dashing up a pine tree. Later in the day I often walked our dog Chance, and Babby would accompany us. Occasionally as we ambled through the neighborhood park we were graced by the gift of tiny purple wildflowers blooming in the grass.

In the early stage of Babby's dementia, we would talk about the good things we enjoyed, such as some of the hymns we sang at church or a special anthem the choir sang. When Babby and I found a chance to talk about the worship service, I asked him how he liked the songs "On Eagle's Wings" and "His Eye Is On the Sparrow."[3] He smiled when I mentioned them and almost teared up, saying they filled a special place in his heart, bringing back good memories. "Me too," I agreed, adding that I had requested those songs because I knew he especially liked them. That seemed to please Babby. What a debt of gratitude I owe to these two songs.

Before I joined the choir, our new choir director began choosing songs that tugged at me with delight. One Sunday while sitting in the pew with Babby, the song "On Eagle's Wings" filled me with a yearning. How I wanted with all my heart to be singing in the middle of that kind of music! It wasn't enough just to listen to those songs. If only I could sing with the choir! I didn't have much of a voice, but I could carry a tune and make a joyful noise. Maybe the director would let me sing with the choir. *But how could I leave Babby sitting in the pew without me beside him?* For several weeks I wrestled with that question, wondering what I should do, asking God to show me or tell me. One Sunday when the choir sang a hymn titled "The Hiding Place"[4] by Jehoiada Brewer, the yearning in my heart grew. Yet I still didn't have a peace about singing with the choir while Babby sat alone.

While I struggled with what to do during the next few weeks, the organist encouraged me to join the choir, and that nudged me to pray about it even more. Finally I heard God say clearly in my mind, *Put Babby in My hands and don't worry about him. I'll take care of him and he won't be alone. You go sing.* That was the joyful green light I needed!

Singing in the choir was refreshing, even during the hard times. Throughout our dementia journey, every time I went to choir practice and every time I sang in church with the choir, God lifted me up and renewed me, no matter how tired I felt. Even though I had to work hard to learn the music, choir time always turned into an uplifting gift. Maybe that was because I focused on singing to the Lord with grateful joy for His sustaining, amazing grace. Maybe it was because our choir director always began and ended choir rehearsal with prayer, asking God to use our talents and gifts of music for His purposes, and lifting up our personal prayer concerns. Maybe it was because choir members and the director enjoyed the fellowship of singing together. And maybe it was because God's Spirit seemed to sing with us and through us, sharing His joy in us and in our songs.

That seemed to make us sound much bigger and better than we thought we could be! This happened especially when we prayed before singing, inviting the Holy Spirit to sing through us, highlighting the wondrous beauty and the message of the music.

After I joined the choir, Babby was always content to sit in the pew without me and listen during Sunday worship, or stand and sing the hymns along with the congregation.

Every time I went to choir practice on Wednesday night, I asked God to take care of Babby at home. When I returned, he would either be sitting in his chair in the living room with our little dog in his lap, or watching TV in the den, or eating ice cream in the kitchen. Thanks be to God!

I continued to be grateful for these contented times, as well as the times when Babby hugged me and told me he loved me. Also I treasured the times he told me I was beautiful even with my hair scrambling wild. But I wondered if these times would fade away. I forecasted that eventually his dementia would drown those endearing words and warm hugs. Still, I determined to love him out of the overflow of our Lord's love, no matter what. And I could ask others to renew their prayers for us. I realized that even though dementia may eclipse his spoken love, even though one day he may not even recognize me, I could still cherish the dear man I fell in love with years earlier.

I didn't know what the future held. Does anyone? But I knew God held the future. As Isaiah 12:2 says in the Bible, "I will trust in him and not be afraid. The LORD GOD is my strength and my song."[5]

Help me trust You, Lord! Let Your strength and Your song carry us on the wings of Your embracing presence.

4

THERAPY LIFELINES

Talking with friends and family via email, or sometimes by phone, became therapy lifelines for me. I've learned by experience that sharing good times multiplies the joy, and sharing burdens divides the load.

About three months after Babby started taking his medication for dementia and people started praying for us, I emailed a friend saying that Babby was doing wonderfully well. "It's amazing! No, God is amazing! Thank you so much for your prayers. I'm sure God is using them. I'm going to keep writing for the newspaper about how God is helping us. I want to praise God for what He has done and is doing. Come to think of it, praise is good therapy, isn't it, whether it is sung or written? Anyway, I believe God will use it for good, even when it's hard to write about. At the very least, it's generated some hugs from friends. And Babby is so generous with his hugs, far more often than before dementia clouded his mind. I have so much to be thankful for! Babby's due back from prison soon, so I'd better scoot and fix some soup for us. Isn't it great that he can continue his prison ministry at Autry (State Prison)! He's always loved volunteering with Prison Fellowship."

Continuing the email conversation with my friend which included a discussion about tragedies described in the Bible compared to my life, I commented, "As you said, no tragedy or ruination is beyond His redeeming joy! Now I see that is what our Lord has done and is doing in my life. My cup overflows, even in the midst of heartaches and struggles, in sickness and in health, for richer or for poorer, our Lord brings joy in many different ways, lightens the load, dispels the darkness."

Two examples illustrate how God redeemed our difficulties during Babby's dementia struggles: First, Babby's anger erupted when I began working on the Prison Fellowship's *Angel Tree* ministry project which provides Christmas presents to children in the name of their incarcerated parent. This volunteer work had been Babby's job until he became too confused in his early dementia fog. When he exploded, thinking I was taking his job away from him, I walked away into the kitchen, wondering how I was going to manage. *He can't do that work any more,* I thought, *but the impoverished families need it, especially the children.* As I pondered this, I heard in my mind: *Fear not, for I am with you.* I relaxed and smiled, knowing God would work it out. Later I realized those words were from a Scripture passage in Isaiah 41:10 that continues, "...for I am your God. I will strengthen you and help you. I will hold you up with my victorious right hand."[1]

Later I worked on the prison ministry Christmas project when Babby was asleep, or taking a walk, or when he was serving at the weekly prison ministry with others. It was apparent to me that God helped me get everything done by the deadline including buying the presents, wrapping them in bright Christmas paper, and labeling each one according to whether they were for a boy or girl, and the age of each child. Most amazing, Babby thanked me for all my hard work (another sign of

God's load-lifting grace). I hugged Babby, thanking God in my heart.

The second example of God's grace concerned an incident during Holy Communion at church. Babby had assisted our pastor with serving Holy Communion for years. But one Sunday Babby experienced difficulties, even dropping some of the bread on the carpeted floor, and he seemed confused about what he needed to do. Nevertheless, he kept repeating the words of Jesus, "This is My body, broken for you," as he offered the broken bread to members of the congregation kneeling at the altar rail.

At our Wednesday night supper that week our pastor found a way to mention the problem to me out of earshot of Babby. "Please pray about this situation and what to do about it. Should I ask someone else to help with Communion or what?" He didn't want to hurt Babby's feelings if someone else took over the job he considered his. While I was pondering this at supper, a member of the congregation told me quietly, "I hope Babby can continue to help serve Communion for as long as he is able. He does it with such a spiritual gentleness." That touched my heart. Nevertheless, Babby's problems couldn't be ignored. A week or so later our pastor told me he decided to ask someone else to assist him with Communion, a decision I supported. At the next Communion Sunday, Babby didn't seem to notice that someone else was doing what had been his role. He never mentioned it. Once again God took care of it.

Of course God's way was not always a smooth way by any means! It was a difficult struggle, but God always found a way to give Babby and me a peace that passes understanding, and to lift my spirits. Choir rehearsals, for instance, continued to restore my soul and my sanity.

What's more, I discovered an unexpected joy that helped ease my heartache: I found that I loved Babby more than before. That was God's gift too, not of my own doing, that's for sure.

Prayer, my own and other people's, provided another lifeline. I especially needed all the prayer I could get when Babby's bouts of irrational anger increased in frequency, catching me by surprise. One night I encountered an onslaught of Babby's anger after he had gone to bed. When I slipped into bed beside him, he startled me by snarling, "Get out!" I calmly replied that the bed was as much mine as his, and I needed my sleep as much as he did. That seemed to infuriate him. He threw back the covers and got up, stomping to the open bedroom door, lurking beside it like a mountain lion guarding his lair. I waited awhile, but when he didn't come back to bed, I got up and walked past him, not knowing if he would grab me, or what. He didn't move, but continued guarding the door, glowering. It was getting late, but I telephoned our son David, explaining the situation and asking for prayer. To my surprise, I wasn't frightened, just concerned, knowing we needed extra prayer. God brought sweet peace as David and I prayed together on the phone, lightening the load and giving me peace. After awhile Babby went back to bed and fell asleep, the anger forgotten. Another answer to prayer! Silently thanking God, I slipped back into bed, smiling. Sleep gently swept over me, another small miracle.

    Another time God used choir practice, along with an anthem we were learning, plus an email conversation to counter what could have caused gnawing anxiety. That Wednesday night, choir rehearsal was especially refreshing, invigorating, and fun. I hadn't laughed so much in a long time. "I needed that," I emailed Ben, our choir director. "I had asked the Lord to perk me up, and He used choir rehearsal to lift me and let me soar. I think the anthem we're working on is delightful!" I wrote. "However, while God was at work in our spirited singing, I think the devil was at work at home," I continued in the email. "When I got home, Babby proceeded to tell me that someone, probably two people, tried to knock down the back door to our laundry room. I don't know what to make of that. But I don't believe it. Was he having a delusion? I don't know. Maybe he heard the noise of a car door slamming at our neighbor's house. Or maybe our cat was outside trying to get someone to let her in. But she never comes to that door. Then on top of that, he got angry about another much smaller detail which I didn't understand. He hasn't been angry like that in a long time. I'm trying not to take it too seriously. Probably tomorrow he will be back to his usual sweet self."

Then I added, "Can you think of any Scripture I can hang my hopes on? Pray for us, will you? That will help, I know." I concluded, "By His Grace."

Ben answered my email the next day. "Sounds like you're doing fine with the unwelcome guests (the anger and the mystery at the back door), too. I like the Psalm 91 reference to God covering us with his feathers, so we can trust Him under his wings. I remember hearing a story about a woman who was stopped by a mugger after she'd just heard a sermon on that verse. She just stood there saying, 'I'm covered with feathers, I'm covered with feathers,' and the mugger ran away."

Ben concluded his email by writing, "You know that a 'great cloud of witnesses' is surrounding you and Babby, and God himself is looking out for you." That boosted my trust in God once again!

Also some of the songs we sang in choir spoke a personal message to me. "So glad we sang, 'Take Up Thy Cross', by Charles Everest," I told Ben in another email. "When we rehearsed it Wednesday night, God seemed to reassure me with the second verse: 'Take up thy cross, let not its weight fill thy weak spirit with alarm; his strength shall bear thy spirit up, and brace thy heart and nerve thine arm.'[2]

"God reaffirmed that message this morning at the worship service," I continued in the email, "and it encouraged me. I don't know why I thought I had to take up my cross and walk alone. Of course the Spirit of our Lord will go with me and help me with His strength! I just needed reminding."

"As far as Babby is concerned," I added, "small signs give me hope that Babby's mind is still somewhat intact, as well as his sense of humor. Yesterday he cracked a wacky joke, and another time he gave me a spontaneous hug, something he hadn't done in quite a while. The hymn, 'Love Lifted Me'[3] by James Rowe, kept singing through my mind and heart all day. Thank the Lord!"

5

Dangerous Driving

*L**ord, I know I asked for a sign, but this is scary, even downright dangerous!*

I had asked the Lord to show me when I should take away Babby's car key. Maybe I should have done that after we survived his erratic driving on our trip to North Georgia to visit our son and his family. His driving then nearly scared the wits out of me. But when we got home he seemed to be able to drive all right along familiar roads with little traffic.

DEALING WITH DEMENTIA

After he had been diagnosed with early stage dementia, he had responded extremely well to the medication his doctor prescribed. Even so, I discovered the hard way that he could not handle driving on busy roads anymore. I had known the time would come when it would not be safe for him to drive at all, even on familiar two-lane roads. Wanting Babby to drive as long as he safely could, I asked God to give me a sign when his driving days should come to an end. The medication was helping even beyond expectations, but I knew the progression of the disease would eat away those gains at some point. I asked God to help me handle the car key situation with respect and love.

God's sign was more than I bargained for when I asked Babby to drive me to Thomasville, a town about 30 miles away, to get my driver's license renewed. My driver's license had expired months earlier, I discovered to my surprise and dismay, and I did not want to risk driving with an expired license.

Babby never had any trouble driving on the familiar four-lane highway to Thomasville before, even after the onset of his brain disease. I decided he should be able to drive me there to get my license renewed.

However, I realized too late that while he drove easily to Thomasville itself, he was not familiar with the exact location of the State Patrol Office. When I pointed to the turn he should take, confusion descended upon him like a fog, blinding his sense of judgment as he turned into the face of oncoming traffic. He avoided a collision by inches, maneuvering onto the side of the road just in time. But the near collision wracked my nerves. I silently told the Lord that if He would get us home safely, I would take away his car key. I knew I had my sign, as scary as it was.

After I renewed my license, I didn't tell him about my decision. We walked out of the State Patrol's office together and I simply got in the driver's seat as Babby got in the passenger seat without comment. Maybe he was relieved he didn't have to drive after nearly having a wreck, if he even remembered the incident. Or maybe he was as scared as I had been. In any case I was thankful that I didn't have to argue with him about my driving us home. Until that point, he always did the driving when we went anywhere together in the car.

That night I couldn't sleep. God seemed to tell me that now was a good time to get Babby's car key and put it away where he couldn't find it. So I did. The next time Babby wanted to drive somewhere locally, he noticed that his key was not in the place where he always kept it, and he asked me about it. Taking a deep breath, I told him that I didn't think it was safe for him to drive any more, and I had put his key away. Trying not to belabor the point by noting various examples, I explained that there were just too many dangerous situations he could come up against driving our car. I did not expect Babby to understand this. Amazingly, he did not argue or question me. He simply accepted the situation, never asking to drive again. In fact, he was wonderfully gracious about it, letting me drive us without any complaints, and not even making "back seat" driving comments. By God's amazing grace, that was one more answer to prayer! I couldn't thank God enough! And I loved my husband all the more.

6

Finding Comfort in a Grocery Store

Lord, please don't let me cry, I pleaded silently as I walked out the door with Babby on our way to church. I knew he didn't mean to snap at me, but it threatened to undo me for a few minutes. Trying to deal with his sometimes roller-coaster symptoms at home, I often lurched between fearful discouragement and uplifting gratitude for Babby's occasional expressions of appreciation.

As I told a friend, he was acting more irritable than he had been in awhile. Maybe he was a little depressed. On the other hand, when I helped him with something like tying his shoelaces, a task that was getting too hard for him, Babby said gratefully, "What would I do without you?" That's when my heart soared, renewing my strength for a time.

But there came a time when I didn't feel well. Maybe I was simply feeling overwhelmed. Going to my Bible, I heard God speak to me in Isaiah 43:

"When you go through rivers of difficulty, you will not drown . . . because you are precious to me . . . and I love you. Do not be afraid, for I am with you."[1]

I reviewed the passage several times, trying to soak up this reassurance. I needed God's peace and I didn't want to be afraid. But tense anxiety still kept me tied up in knots too often.

Mulling over my struggle to find some sense of peace, I suddenly remembered something that happened a year or two earlier when Babby's oldest sister died at her home in Tennessee after fighting Alzheimer's disease for several years. The whole drawn-out situation haunted me during her struggles. I loved Tena and hated hearing how her mind and body were slowly failing. And of course I couldn't help but think how her pathway foreshadowed Babby's situation. When she died, I wondered how I could make the trip with Babby from our home in South Georgia to Tennessee for the funeral. I was relieved and grateful when our son David said he would drive us. What a difference that made!

During our visitation with the family before and after his sister's funeral, I made awkward attempts to console those grieving, while trying to help Babby with his bewilderment. At the same time I felt a surreal sense of love that held us together in our shared grief. That comforted me.

Returning home from the funeral, we resumed our usual habits that helped keep us going. That included attending church on Sunday. As usual, I sang in the choir. After the church service a friend gave me a comforting hug. It made me think of God hugging me, giving me hope.

As that memory tugged at my heart, God seemed to speak softly in my mind: *Let Me embrace you and Babby with My wrap-around perfect love. Lean on Me and soak up My enduring love, My empowering love, My strength, My peace that passes understanding. I will not fail you or Babby.*

I shut my eyes and relaxed, leaning in relief on those reassuring words of promise. Taking a deep breath, I smiled, realizing that the words I had heard in my heart and mind were based on the passage in the Bible which was quoted that morning in church.

"Love never gives up, never loses faith, is always hopeful, and endures through every circumstance... Three things will last forever — faith, hope, and love — and the greatest of these is love."[2]

Suddenly I understood how God's personal, unfailing love was meant not only to comfort and strengthen us, but also to overflow *through* us like a watering can for others.

Excitedly I emailed this new understanding to our music director, Ben, who had commented on the 1 Corinthians 13 passage in church, highlighting God's empowering love. "My love and strength will fail, but God's won't," I wrote him. "Now I understand that Christ's indwelling presence empowers me to love Babby in ways I never could on my own. I hadn't realized before how Christ's love empowers me. That's a reassuring reality I can latch onto. That was God speaking to me through your pulpit comments. I'm grateful for that. It helps me handle these difficulties."

I asked him for any other Scripture or comments he could apply to my situation. "I need all the help I can get," I added.

In response, Ben reminded me that God's word says to us, "'My strength [God's strength] is made perfect in your weakness,'"³ he quoted 2 Corinthians 12:9. Then he added, "What to do, when the going goes beyond our strength and comforts? We keep laying our weakness before Him to perfect it into strength. Lord, thank you for leading Joanne today," he prayed for me in the email. "Thank you even for the exhaustion and fear she feels, because in Jesus, when we know that we are weak, then we can become strong, because the fullness of the Godhead dwells in Christ, and Christ in us."

I doubted if I could thank the Lord for the exhaustion and fear I often felt, but somehow his prayer for me gave me a sense of peace anyway. Later, after thinking about what he wrote, I realized that I can ask the Lord to strengthen me and reassure me, thanking Him that He promised to do just that because He cares for us. He will not fail or forsake us, as He promised, thank the Lord! I just have to keep asking, and keep trusting in the peace that passes understanding which only He can give.

However, that peace shattered a day or two later when something happened that shook me to the core. Babby was about to go to the Post Office to mail a small item when I asked him a question about it. Without any warning, he exploded, grabbed my wrist with frightening strength and yelled at me! As soon as he saw the stricken look on my face he let go of me. I walked away into the kitchen on the verge of tears. *Is this the way it's going to be, Lord?* I asked silently. I was shaken by how fast it happened, like lightning out of a cloudless sky with no warning thunder. I knew it was the disease causing him to act that way, and not the man I married years ago, but my hands still trembled.

To my surprise, he followed me into the kitchen. I stiffened, not knowing what to expect. "Can you forgive me?" he asked. I could only nod my head yes with tentative relief. This incident troubled me for several days, as I wondered what might happen next. Were we on a downward spiral? Where was my peace now? Could God work good out of what I might be facing?

A few days later I received an unexpected answer. Sunday after church Babby and I walked a few blocks to a local restaurant called Grandma's Kitchen. I felt like singing when Babby's hand found mine, and we walked hand in hand as a delightful summer breeze chased away the oppressive heat while the sun took a snooze behind merciful clouds.

Inside the cafeteria style restaurant, ceiling fans kept the breeze stirring. Getting in line for the buffet, I stood behind a man who looked familiar, but I didn't think I knew him. He turned to me and told me he enjoyed reading my columns in the newspaper about our dementia struggle because they encouraged him. "Makes me realize we're not alone in our troubles, and know that other people have problems too. Reading about the way God helps you, helps me. We especially needed that encouragement last week when my wife was going through a hard time."

Wow! Those affirming words gave me such a lift! I had no doubt that God arranged for me to walk up behind that man, and for him to share those words! Gratitude filled my heart to overflowing. That man's thankful words blew away all my sadness!

God used a similar encounter at a grocery store not long after that to bless and encourage me again. As I scurried up and down the aisles picking up needed items, I exchanged greetings with an elderly gentleman I'd seen several times but didn't know personally. Shortly afterward, he came up to me, smiling a little. "I just want to tell you how one of your newspaper articles especially helped me," he said. His wife has Alzheimer's disease, he told me. He takes care of her at home with the help of two ladies who come at different times of the day. He and his wife have been married sixty years, he said, and now she is in her seventh year with Alzheimer's. They had both worked hard all their lives and saved money to use for enjoying their golden years. "I get so depressed sometimes," he repeated several times. "But when it gets me down too much I get out your story that quoted the hymn, 'Turn Your Eyes Upon Jesus.'[4] I cut it (the article) out of the paper and keep it where I can read it again," he said. The song comforts him, he indicated, and helped him keep going. "Turn your eyes upon Jesus," he quoted again softly. "Thank you for writing that."

Deeply moved, I couldn't resist hugging him, thanking him for telling me this. "You've blessed me so much," I told him.

He did indeed bless me more than he knew. For one thing, I badly needed to be reminded to turn *my* eyes upon Jesus. Babby had gotten worse, which wasn't surprising since he was in his fifth year with dementia at the time. Too often I got caught up in the tiring, depressing details of taking care of him. Don't get me wrong. I was grateful that I could still take care of him at home. But sometimes, like the kind gentleman I met in the store, I let the demands of caregiving get me down. Sometimes I forgot to look to the source of my strength and comfort. I found it illuminating that that the composer, Helen H. Lemmel, who wrote music and lyrics of the hymn, "Turn Your Eyes Upon Jesus," was blind when she wrote it, and suffered more than her share of struggles and heartache. In the song she wrote:

> "O soul, are you weary and troubled?
> No light in the darkness you see?
> There's light for a look at the Savior,
> And life more abundant and free!
>
> Turn your eyes upon Jesus,
> Look full in His wonderful face,
> And the things of earth will grow strangely dim,
> In the light of His glory and grace."[5]

The gentleman's words in the grocery store lifted me up in another way. They told me that God was using my writing to help others as He helped me. That thrilled me! And besides, it was good therapy for me to tell how God's grace was sufficient for me and sustained me during those trying times. No doubt God arranged these specific encouraging encounters.

7
GIFT OF HOPE

Cancer a gift of hope? How could a diagnosis of skin cancer open the door to hope concerning Babby's dementia? Cancer and dementia are two different diseases that have nothing to do with each other, right? It sounds strange, but my husband's diagnosis of skin cancer did lead to a path of hope concerning his dementia.

It happened this way: A strange-looking lump appeared on the back of Babby's left hand and showed no signs of diminishing, raising my suspicions it might be cancer. I took him to our family doctor. When he confirmed that the lump was cancer, our doctor said the good news was that the cancer was not the kind that usually spreads to the lymph nodes or elsewhere, unless it goes unchecked for a long time. It did need to be surgically removed, he said, but that could be done in his office using a local anesthesia. It would take only an hour or so.

I was relieved and grateful. Before setting up the appointment for that surgery, the doctor asked me how Babby was getting along in general. I told him I thought he was doing remarkably well, considering everything, because he had been on the same plateau for months and months without getting any worse. He was still able to do the same things he could do the year before, without any noticeable change.

"Hmm," his doctor said, sounding like he had stumbled across a clue to a puzzle he had not seen before. Flipping through Babby's chart back to when he was first diagnosed with "some kind of dementia," in late 2005, he spotted a notation that didn't seem significant at the time. Soon after the diagnosis, he had ordered a CT scan of Babby's brain to see if he had had any small strokes. The scan ruled that out, but the scan did reveal "small vascular changes," according to the notation. "You know," the doctor said, thinking out loud, "people with Alzheimer's type dementia show changes for the worse every few months. But people who have vascular dementia reach a plateau and stay there for a long time. When they do lose some abilities, they stay at that level for some time as well. I believe he has vascular dementia."

As the doctor explained, with vascular dementia, changes in tiny blood vessels in the brain gradually act like tiny blockages that are not perceptible at first, but over time, in stages, they erode short-term memories, words, names even of loved ones, emotions, and physical abilities. At the time I didn't fully realize how extensive this could be long term, and sometimes how heartbreaking. For instance, there eventually came a time when Babby could not remember the names of our two sons or other close family members, although if I mentioned their names he seemed to remember who they were, and smile. He adored our sons; they were his pride and joy. As for their wives and our grandchildren, he seemed to have no recollection of them at all.

There came a time later when we could no longer hold even a simple conversation at meal times or any other time. I would say something, or ask him a question, and he would give me a bewildered look as if I were speaking a foreign language. Patiently repeating the question or asking him a more simple, straightforward question seemed to have no different effect. "I can't...seem...right now...I think...all those folks...you know," Babby would stammer with long pauses in between. Or on occasion, when the words simply would not come, we ate together in exhausted silence.

Physically, his walking became a slanting shuffle. One day he came home from a short walk, leaning to one side. Even when he sat down in a chair he leaned to one side. Still, he loved walking outdoors, even if his gait tripped him up sometimes, and he could only walk slowly. Two or three times he fell, stumbling over uneven ground or sidewalk. I was not strong enough to help him get up, but one time a man nearby saw him fall and came to help. Another time he fell in our yard and I ran inside the house to call our pastor who lived a block away. Thank heavens he was at home. He came right over and helped Babby into our house. Thank God for good neighbors. Also I was thankful that Babby never hurt himself when he fell.

When his doctor diagnosed Babby's disease as vascular dementia rather than Alzheimer's, I latched my hopes onto the "plateau" of little or no changes which the doctor said could last a long time. That gave me the hope he would not get really bad for several months or years, especially compared to Alzheimer's patients. That hope for me meant Babby might not have to go to a nursing home, or if he did, it would be only for a short time before he went to heaven. For Babby's sister, Tena, who struggled with dementia until the end of her life, her physical abilities remained intact, at a rudimentary level at least. Her husband Bob was able to take care of her at home until a couple of months before she died.

I'm deeply grateful that I didn't know how bad things would get before Babby died in 2009. The strain of dreading and worrying about how I could handle future situations would have piled an unbearable burden on the present day's situations even when that day's burden was relatively light. Blessings of the better days would have been lost to me in worrying about harder days to come. Focusing on the good of each day no matter how small and giving thanks enabled me to see signs of God's caring, loving kindness even in the harder days that did come. Those signs sometimes came through the unexpected kindness of a stranger or a friend and through the supportive prayers of people who lifted us up. At times I could feel those prayers holding us close in His comfort.

At the same time I was acutely aware that vascular dementia is a terrible, progressive disease with no cure. I didn't want to minimize it. But I was thankful Babby responded well to the medication, at least in the beginning stage. The hope and peace God gave me simply reassured me that God is taking care of us no matter how difficult things might get. What's more, knowing we were in His loving care, I felt blessed to be able to take care of Babby in the comfort and strength God gave me at home.

8
His Name Is Fear

Oh God, what if a spinal block is not feasible? What if Babby has to be put to sleep for the surgery? What will happen to his mind?

I couldn't bear to think about it, and yet I couldn't think of anything else. The frightening possibility jerked me awake in the middle of the night. Symptoms of possible prostate cancer had taken us to a specialist his family doctor recommended. When the test results of his prostate biopsy came back, the specialist told us that he did have prostate cancer, and that it had to be treated soon. He needed surgery for a radiation seed implant. The good news: the cancer was in the earliest possible stage, and the treatment is highly effective.

But the crucial question for me was, "Does he have to be put to sleep for the surgery?" As I explained to the specialist, my husband had dementia. I didn't want general anesthesia putting him to sleep to cause a setback. The doctor answered my uptight question by saying anesthesia was required for the surgical procedure. He must have seen the panic-stricken look on my face because he hastened to add that a spinal block might be a possibility instead of anesthesia. He left to call an anesthesiologist to check on that. When he returned he said the anesthesiologist wanted to discuss the options with us, so we scheduled an appointment in two weeks with him.

Focusing on a possible spinal block option that would allow him to be awake during the surgical procedure, I tensely talked myself into a tentative peace about it for a couple of days. Then I woke up with the frightening "what if" questions whirling through my mind, worrying about what might happen to his mind if he had to be completely sedated for the surgery. Babby had reached a plateau stage in his disease, and I couldn't bear to think that the anesthesia might send him into a downward spiral in his already diminished cognitive abilities. When I asked the doctors about it, they couldn't give me any answers, much less any assurance. They simply didn't know how Babby might respond mentally to being put to sleep.

The morning after I wrestled most of the night with fear, I woke up a worried wreck. Even praying didn't seem to help. I desperately wanted to talk to someone who could help me find a way to handle this. When I couldn't reach our pastor or his wife on the phone, I decided to once again email an SOS prayer request to Ben, our minister of music. I enjoyed working under his direction in the choir at our church, and admired the way he explained the scriptural basis of the songs and hymns we sang. Besides that, he always encouraged us in kind ways. *Please, God, give him the words I need*, I prayed silently.

My trembling fingers stumbled over the email computer keys as I typed hastily, explaining the situation: "I need your prayers for peace of mind and some reassuring words. I've lost the peace I had about Babby's upcoming surgery because I realized that I was pinning all my hopes on the spinal block as the solution to his avoiding general anesthesia that might cause a permanent setback in his mental condition. If a spinal block is not feasible, where does that leave me? Scared to death! I need to be able to trust our Lord no matter what. Even if Babby has to be put to sleep, I need to trust God to work it out for good for Babby and for me. I've struggled with this half the night. I don't know why I can't just put it in God's hands and trust him. I finally got up at 5:30 this morning and talked to our Lord about this in my prayer journal and listened to him. Also I read Scripture, including what Jesus told his disciples in the Upper Room the night before he was arrested and crucified. All reassuring. But I'm still struggling."

Just writing that email plea for help calmed me down enough to work on a couple of projects while I waited for his answer. But I was shaky when I opened his reply that afternoon. "You've met our enemy, haven't you, and found his name is Fear," he wrote. *He's got that right, I thought.*

"It's no accident that the Incarnation's soundtrack (remember the message of Christmas told by Luke) is punctuated by, 'Don't be afraid' said by the angel Gabriel to Zechariah, Mary, and the shepherds. Jesus suffered death, Hebrews says, to set us free from the fear of death….

Does that mean Christians never experience fear? Nope. Peter walked on the water, then got terrified.

It means that coming face to face with Fear, for Christ's people, is the doorway into deeper fellowship with Jesus – into knowing the perfect love that casts out fear – into experiencing the Thou Art With Me of a loving Shepherd walk through the valley of the shadow of death.

Sounds to me like you're doing exactly the right thing – wrestling. Great assurance, like a great marriage, is built moment by moment.

Yours in the struggle to live fearlessly in Him, Ben."

Relief washed over me. "Thank you, Ben!" I responded in an email. "This helps a lot. Perfect love casts out fear. God's perfect love! Of course! And I had been beating myself up for being so afraid, but I guess I'm in good company. I forgot how many of God's people in the Bible, including Jesus' disciples, wrestled with fear. In fact, I'm just now thinking, Jesus wrestled with fear in the garden before he was arrested, didn't He? And since Jesus lives in my heart and is with me in His Spirit, the victory He won can be my victory, too, right? Even though what I'm facing is nothing compared to what Jesus was facing, still, it means He understands and knows how to help me, wouldn't you say? You've got me thinking in the right direction.

"Thanks too for reminding me of the 23rd Psalm: 'Yea though I walk through the valley of the shadow of death, I will fear no evil... Your rod and Your staff, they comfort me.'[1] That has been such a meaningful reassurance before. I don't know why I didn't think to turn to it. Fear blinded me, I guess.

"I'm going to print this out and re-read it several times to let it all sink in along with other Scripture I found this morning. I can feel myself relaxing a little already. God must have given you the words that pointed me in the direction of peace. Thanks so much!"

I concluded by writing, "Yours clinging to the same Lifeline."

9

WORRY WRESTLING

I took our dog for a walk and cried out to the Lord. *I'm losing him inch by inch! That's hard enough. Emotionally it's a roller coaster and I hate roller coasters! But if I lose his love too, I don't think I can bear that! His mind is slowly fading away. Will his love for me also fade? It's all so overwhelming!*

The peace that had held me calm suddenly crumbled when we went to see the radiologist concerning his upcoming prostate cancer surgery. Since Babby had not seen this doctor before, the nurse asked Babby a barrage of questions during the information process prior to seeing the doctor. The nurse couldn't have been nicer, but apparently the stress of trying to remember the answers fogged up Babby's mind. I had to answer most of the questions for him, even basic ones. That caught me by surprise. I didn't realize his mind had slipped that much, seemingly overnight.

By the time we got home, he was exhausted. Apparently struggling to answer questions he couldn't answer left him drained physically as well as mentally, plus it frayed his emotions. When I asked him about helping out with a chore he had always done in the past, he exploded. It seemed to plunge him backward to the dark days before he began taking his medication for his dementia. His snarling hostility pushed me away as he launched a verbal attack. Devastated, I knew I had to get out of the house. That's when I grabbed our dog's leash and took him for a walk.

Later that day Babby asked me to forgive him, which of course I was glad to do. The next day the storm was over, and he told me he loved me two or three times, and that I was beautiful at least once. I was grateful, but I was still struggling. I didn't know what would happen next, and I couldn't handle the uncertainties. I stayed on the verge of tears.

However, I determined I would not give in to self-pity or despair. I could not afford those traps. I asked our Lord to help me banish these emotions, and instead fill my mind and heart with His promises from the Bible. Immediately I heard His voice in my mind tell me, echoing Scripture,

> "I will never fail you. I will never abandon you."[1]

> "Even when I walk through the darkest valley, I will not be afraid, for you are close beside me."[2]

> "In all these things we are more than conquerors through him who loved us."[3]

> "My grace is all you need. My power works best in weakness."[4]

As I continued to listen in snatches of quiet time, I also heard the Holy Spirit tell me in my mind, "Do not be anxious about tomorrow, for tomorrow will be anxious for itself."[5] I looked that up in the New Testament and found it in Matthew 6:34. Wanting to understand further, I read that same verse in *The Message* version, and heard God speaking directly to me:

> "Give your entire attention to what God is doing right now, and don't get worked up about what may or may not happen tomorrow.

God will help you deal with whatever hard things come up when the time comes."[6]

Then God brought to mind a devotional I had read about visualizing Jesus standing in front of me with His cupped hands outstretched, as if waiting for me to put something in His strong, nail-scarred hands. I gave Him my burdens of worry and fear. To my astonishment, these heavy burdens immediately dissolved, lifting off my shoulders and out of my hands.

One other visual came to my mind. Corrie ten Boom grew up in Holland during World War II and was interred by the Nazis in the Ravensbrück concentration camp. Sadly, her sister and her father, along with other loved ones, died from imprisonment during the final year of the war. In her book, *The Hiding Place,* Corrie ten Boom tells about asking her father, when she was a child, how she could be sure God would give her the strength to face troubles in the uncertain future:

> "Corrie," he began gently, "when you and I go to Amsterdam — when do I give you your ticket?"
>
> "Why, just before we get on the train."
>
> "Exactly. And our wise Father in heaven knows when we're going to need things, too. Don't run out ahead of Him, Corrie. When the time

comes that some of us will have to die, you will look into your heart and find the strength you need — just in time."[7]

During choir practice we sometimes sang a song called, "I Have a Hope,"[8] by Jim Firth. The tune lifted my soul and the lyrics gently pointed me to God's complete, careful and perfect control over my future. And Babby's future. I was reminded that God is a God of Hope — we find living hope in the name of Jesus. I didn't have to worry about when or how Babby would die. Because Jesus offers us a constant spring of living hope, I could drink deeply from the well of peace and hope even in the face of death.

Babby's expressions of love may fade away, I knew. But the Hope we both shared deep in our hearts will never fade away, keeping our love for one another strong in our Lord's unfailing, everlasting love. Our Hope is alive in both of us, I realized, living day to day. Step by step with our Lord, through the storms, through our songs, in our stumbling, in our smiles, in our fears and through the confusing fog, He always holds our hands whether we realize it or not.

Lord, help me remember this no matter what happens, I prayed.

10

Abundant Reassurance

I thought I had prepared myself for the worst possible scenario concerning a surgical procedure scheduled for Babby's prostate cancer, while at the same time hoping for the best. I thought I was already convinced to trust God and stop pinning all my hopes on a spinal block as an alternative to general anesthesia for the cancer surgery because I was afraid the anesthesia could have long term negative effects on Babby's dementia, causing a sudden downward spiral in his cognitive abilities.

God had reassured me through various sources including an email from a friend, through a devotional, through Scripture, through what the author Corrie ten Boom wrote, through songs, and through other things the Spirit had brought to mind. All of that helped tremendously. But as the date for the surgery loomed closer and closer, worry and fear began stalking me all over again.

When we talked to the radiologist, he explained that a spinal block posed a risk that he would not recommend. He assured us that they had done more than 300 radiation seed implants and none had failed, which is very good news. But when I asked if the anesthesia might adversely affect Babby's mind long term, he told me to ask the anesthesiologist about that.

I hate not having all the answers or not knowing what to expect! While waiting almost two weeks to see the anesthesiologist, I struggled, wavering between worry and hope, my mind running in circles.

God intervened again through two telephone calls, as well as more Scripture, prayer, and another song. First of all, while talking on the phone with Steven, a friend who played the organ at our church, I told him I knew God would give me complete peace once I got some answers about the surgery. He quietly replied, "He can give you that peace right now, you know." Of course! It was like a light turning on in my dim brain. I decided right then to ask God for the peace Jesus promised:

> "I am leaving you with a gift — peace of mind and heart. And the peace I give is a gift the world cannot give. So don't be troubled or afraid."[1]

Soon peace and joy overflowed in my heart with laughter and songs we sang at choir practice, and continued to echo in my mind and heart at home. But the next day I stumbled back into my old worrying habit of trying to prepare for bleak possibilities.

Patiently, God sent another message through a relative who called to inquire about Babby. I told her how I had come to realize that even if the anesthesia sets Babby back mentally, and/or Babby could no longer express his love to me which he had been doing lately with delightful affection in warm words and hugs, I believed I could still show my love to him out of the abundant overflow of the love God gives me, along with the love and support showered upon both of us from friends and family. I thought I was being brave, but underneath I was quaking. I could hardly bear the thought of losing Babby's love.

"Let me give you some advice," she interjected. "Don't project into the future. Just take one day at a time. Enjoy the good times, and trust God to give you the strength to deal with the difficult times."

I needed to hear that. She ought to know. A number of years ago she lost her husband to a long battle with cancer. Once again God reassured me through Scripture such as,

> "Don't be afraid, for I am with you. Don't be discouraged, for I am your God. I will strengthen you and help you. I will hold you up with my victorious right hand."[2]

As I visualized the Lord holding me up as we walked through the difficult days, my joy began to soar once again.

I finally had the opportunity to talk with the anesthesiologist in the hospital before Babby was about to undergo the surgical procedure that was designed to make measurements which would guide the surgeon for the actual prostate cancer surgery two or three weeks later. The anesthesiologist could not give us any guarantees about how the surgery would affect Babby mentally because the doctor didn't didn't know how the anesthesia might affect Babby's dementia long term. But to my surprise that uncertainty didn't flip me out in fear about what might happen. Instead, I felt many prayers undergirding us, and Christ's peace holding me steady.

As it turned out, the surgical procedure for the measurements went smoothly. The anesthesiologist had told us, "You will be surprised how quickly the anesthesia wears off." Was I ever! I never dreamed Babby would not be even slightly groggy! Instead, he was hungry! We went straight to Farmers' Table – a buffet restaurant nearby – just two hours after he was sedated. Babby filled his plate full, and ate every bit. When we got home, he was not even tired or sore. Moreover, his mind seemed no worse for wear. I couldn't thank God enough for answering many prayers way beyond what I dared ask or dream!

The actual prostate surgery with the radiation seed implant was scheduled a few weeks later, and would take about an hour, his doctor estimated. In the meantime Babby continued to do remarkably well, handling chores around the house, making me laugh with his wisecracks and wacky sense of humor, and telling me that he loved me at least once a day. I was learning that whenever he burst out in angry spells, to stop and pray for him, often on my knees, and wait on the Lord. Time after time God restored the overflowing love in Babby's heart. As I told a friend, "What's more, God took away all my fear that Babby's love would fade away as I could see his mind fading away. I can't describe the peace the Lord has given me about that."

I also emailed another friend about this latest victory over fear. "It came about during our church's Bible study recently. I shared with the group how I had struggled with the uncertainties of possibly losing Babby's love. At the close of the meeting as we were leaving, one of the women hugged me and whispered in my ear, 'I'm a shy person, and I don't usually talk about God and what He says to me. But as you were talking, He kept nudging me to tell you that you won't lose Babby's love — *ever*. It will always be there. Someday he might not be able to express it verbally,' she said, 'but God will help you see his love, perhaps through a glint in his eyes or some other way.'"

Don't be afraid — just believe, the Spirit urged my heart.

Then this thought came to me: Babby's love will not fade away any more than God's love will fade away, because God's love is in him, and God's love is eternal! Yes, there will be eclipses hiding his love, but underneath his love lives on, even in heaven after he dies to this world.

As we walked out of the Bible study meeting, the woman and I told each other we felt the Spirit's confirmation flow over us like a reassuring hug. I heard Him whisper, *I'm here with you, working all things for good.*

    I wrote in my prayer journal, "I do believe, Lord! I do believe with all my heart. Thank you, thank you, Lord! I can't thank You enough! I want to hug you and dance before you with all my might."

    Another amazing gift of assurance He gave me was when He melted my fear of the long-term effects of the anesthesia. As I emailed a friend, "It's in God's hands, just as Babby and I are in His hands. So there's no reason to worry! God has worked everything else out in uncertain times before. I'm sure He will continue to do that, one way or another. Does this mean I'll never be afraid again? No. But I think I can now more easily ask Him to restore my peace, and trust that He will. I still need all the prayers and help I can get, and I always will, I'm sure. Often I feel so fatigued. But what God told Paul in the New Testament is so true today: 'My grace is sufficient for you, for my power is made perfect in weakness.'[3] That was God speaking to me, too, for sure!" I concluded. Sharing this encouraging truth with my friend in the email reinforced it in my heart and gave me renewed hope.

    Babby came through his radiation seed implant surgery according to plans with just one hitch – his throat went into spasms during the surgery requiring a second tube to help him breathe. That did not affect the surgery itself, thank God; it just prolonged the recovery for a while to make sure everything was back in order. Our pastor came and prayed with us before Babby was taken to the operating room. After our pastor left, one of Babby's friends from the prison ministry came to check on his progress. That was shortly after I learned about Babby's spasms, so I was glad to have someone to talk and pray with during that time.

We were able to get home around 4:00 p.m. Our son Hollis had arrived that afternoon from North Carolina to help out after the surgery. I was grateful that he was there to drive us home from the hospital because I was exhausted.

Babby experienced a sore throat for about two or three days after the surgery, but there was no pain anywhere else. I was amazed because two probes were used containing hundreds of needles that the surgical team used to insert the radiation seeds.

The third day after the surgery he spent half an hour or more mowing our grass. That took significant strength because, as usual, he pushed our old fashioned non-motorized mower.

The best news of all was that the anesthesia did not set him back mentally. Thanks be to God!

Oh yes, I also praised and thanked God for holding me in His steady, strong peace. I didn't feel a trace of anxiety! God's peace never left me during the surgery. He reminded me that, "I can do all things through Christ who strengthens me,"[4] as God promises in Philippians 4:13. He showed me that He will give me what I need when I need it, and He will deliver me from whatever threatens to defeat or divert me from His purpose and plans.

11

PEOPLE-ANGELS

I never would have dreamed that angels live in our small town until Babby encountered some who helped us both. These were not angels with wings, but I think of them as "people-angels." Because our town is small, people tend to know each other, and what's more, they care. I wrote about our dementia experiences and contributed them to our local newspaper as a weekly editorial column, although I had retired from my journalist job a few years prior. Soon I noticed that these articles helped many citizens of our town become aware of our situation. As Babby walked around town — occasionally getting lost — people recognized him and they knew to call me if I needed to go get him and bring him home.

Even breakfast, which I prefer to skip, became for Babby a blessing time involving a few ordinary men who acted like helpful, friendly angels. Every morning except Sunday, Babby walked about three blocks from our home to Tank & Tummy — a local gas station converted into a diner — for breakfast, eating with several retired men who welcomed him to their table.

One morning shortly after Babby left the house and headed for Tank & Tummy, Fred, the manager, called me. He said that Babby had fallen outside his business, tripping on something in the parking lot. His face had hit an object that caused some bleeding around one eye. Fred said he called the fire department located only two short blocks away. The responders cleaned the wound, stopped the bleeding, and placed a large bandage on his face.

"Should I come get him?" I asked Fred.

"He's inside eating breakfast now and seems fine," Fred replied. "If he gets dizzy or acts confused, I'll call you back. I just wanted to let you know what happened to prepare you when you see him banged up with a big bandage on his face."

A little later, Babby walked home unassisted, and the wound healed in a few days. How thankful I was for Fred who called the fire department to help Babby, then thoughtfully called me. Also I was grateful for the paramedics, plus the men who always invited Babby to their table.

Another time I got a telephone call from a man who made deliveries for Moye's Drug Store, a small hometown pharmacy. He told me that he spotted Babby in the parking lot at a lawyer's office on Curry Street. "He didn't look too good," he said, explaining that Babby was "kinda staggering around" between telephone poles in the parking lot. "If I didn't know better, I would have thought he was drunk," he said.

"I'll come get him," I told him, thanking him for calling. I drove past the law office but saw no sign of Babby. Growing more concerned, I circled the block. Finally I spotted him a little farther down the road. Stopping, I offered him a ride. He seemed glad to see me, and to my relief, he had no trouble getting into the car or walking after we got home.

"Babby, what happened?" I asked. He said he had walked down Curry Street, past his childhood home where he was born, then turned around to walk home. When he got near the law office, his legs didn't want to work right, he said, and he felt tired and weak. He leaned against the light poles near the law office, first one pole, then another. After a while he resumed walking, step by difficult step. When Babby made it a short distance further to Anderson's Cleaners, the owner — who just happened to be near the front of his business that day and saw him — came out and invited him inside to rest, which Babby did. A few minutes later he felt strong enough to continue. He had gone only a few feet from there when I picked him up. After that time he never seemed to experience any similar trouble with his legs "not working right" until a year or more later as his dementia worsened. I thanked God for the man who alerted me and for the man who invited him inside his business to rest. Both acted like helpful angels.

Another morning I received a call from a woman at a small grocery store located several blocks away from Babby's usual route. She said she noticed a man she thought might be Babby behind her store, and went to check on him. Confirming his identity, she warned him that the neighborhood he was in was not safe.

As she told me, "Sometimes there are boys who deal drugs back there. They might knock him on the head for his wallet." When I drove to the store, she told me she had called the police to see about him. "An officer found him a few blocks away near the old saw mill, and said Mr. Hand explained that he was taking his daily walk," she said the policeman told her. With those words echoing in my mind, I went to look for him, praying as I drove, urgently asking God to protect him and to help me find him.

After driving up and down the streets in that run-down neighborhood without seeing him, I finally decided to see if he had somehow made it home. To my relief, I found him slowly trudging toward our house, almost in our yard. When we got in the house, I told him I heard he had been in dangerous territory. He grinned, saying, "That's what several people told me." We talked about it for a while, but he didn't remember being overly confused or concerned while walking. To him, it was just part of his morning walk. Had he gotten lost? Perhaps, but I'm not sure. Although he admittedly had gotten a little off his normal path, Babby was just exploring the town he grew up in.

Another morning after Babby had been gone on a walk for an hour or two, a lady came knocking on my door at our house. She looked familiar, but I couldn't remember her name. She said, "I don't want to barge into your business, Joanne, but did you know Babby is out walking near Cotton

Avenue? (This was a little more than a mile away from our house.) I told her it was all right because he was doing so well, and often walked that far or further. She just wanted to make sure he wasn't lost, she said. "That could be a frightening thing," adding that a relative of hers had Alzheimer's, and she was familiar with some of the symptoms, one of which is wandering away and getting lost. She just wanted to make sure he was all right. She also said she thought it was good that I was writing about it in the newspaper, "because nearly everyone knows of someone with dementia, and what you write helps and encourages all of us."

That was such an encouragement to me. I believe God sent her. She went out of her way to come by our house as she was going to work, and I was so grateful she would do that. I needed an unexpected word of encouragement for now, and for the future, to be reminded that God's angels, including "people-angels," are looking after us. Also it was gratifying to know that God was using my writing to help and encourage others the way He has helped and encouraged me. I am convinced that many small towns, suburbs and cities are populated with just the right number of "people-angels," and I am so blessed to have met a few of them!

This was reinforced when another lady I didn't know called me on the phone a few days later. "I saw Babby walking toward Highway U.S. 19. He was close to the highway, and I know he shouldn't be out that far," she told me, voicing her concern.

This time it sounded like Babby had definitely veered way off course and perhaps was lost. As I explained to her, Babby had told me that morning that he was headed for the Georgia Power office — which was nowhere near Highway U.S. 19 — to deliver a check to pay our bill. "He must have gotten confused and lost his way," I replied. "Thank you for calling! I'll go get him."

Babby's doctor had warned me that one day Babby would get lost. By this time he had struggled with dementia for about three years. It's about half a mile from our house to the Georgia Power office, by a zig-zagged walking route. He had walked to Georgia Power dozens of times previously, but before he left that morning with the check he said he wasn't too sure how to get there. That should have clued me that his walking there was not a good idea this time, especially on a hot summer day. But when I described the route and location of the office, he seemed to remember, and wanted to go. He always wanted to be helpful.

Hanging up the telephone, I hurried to the car praying, *Oh Lord, help me to find him! Please guide me!* Heading for U.S. 19 at the north intersection, I turned south, scanning the sidewalk and every turnoff on the way. Not seeing him, I turned onto another road, then followed a fork in the road toward the Georgia Power building, praying harder than ever.

Finally I spotted him trudging along a road leading toward town, a couple of blocks away from Georgia Power. The check was not peeking out of his shirt pocket where he had placed it. I eased the car beside him and rolled down the window. "Want a ride?" I asked. He grinned, happy to see me. I asked him if he had taken the check to Georgia Power, and he nodded, patting his empty shirt pocket.

Repeating my invitation for a ride, he came close and said, "If it's all right with you, I'd like to walk home." That surprised me, but since he was headed in the right direction, I didn't want to discourage him, and told him I would see him at home. I figured if he didn't show up in a fairly short period of time, I'd know where to look. A few minutes after I got home he walked in our door. I breathed a prayer of thanksgiving. He didn't remember getting lost or being concerned.

Once again, God sent his "angels" to look after Babby and me. Furthermore, it blessed my heart that Babby wanted to serve and care for me, looking for ways to help around the house, and even surprising me with an affectionate hug for no reason other than to encourage me. I believe it must bless God's heart, too, when all his children — especially his "people-angels"— patiently go out of their way to serve others — even strangers.

12

More People-Angels

I believed that as long as Babby could walk, no matter how slow or wobbly, I could take care of him at home, with God's help. His vascular dementia affected his balance as well as his brain, but somehow God kept him, and me, going. When I took our small dog Chance for his daily walks, Babby liked to go with us, but it proved to be a challenge. For our energetic dog, going on walks meant straining at his leash as he excitedly followed his nose from one sniffing spot to the next. For Babby, it was all a very slow, wobbly plod, which meant he inevitably got further and further behind as Chance pulled and urged me forward. I wanted to walk beside Babby, holding his hand, but it was just too hard to coordinate both dog and Babby. Nevertheless, my persistent husband usually kept within sight of me and Chance as he followed behind us.

Babby did fall a couple of times on our walks. The first time he fell we were across the street from Allen's BP gas station — a family owned business. Babby wasn't hurt by his fall, but I wasn't strong enough to help him get up. Before I could yell for help, Allen, the proprietor, rushed over and gently helped Babby get back up on his feet. I was amazed that Allen just happened to see our plight because usually he was preoccupied working on a vehicle inside the service station bays, or he was pumping gas for a customer. He easily could have missed seeing Babby on the ground needing help across the street. As far as I was concerned, Allen was an angel — a people-angel — sent by God.

The second time Babby fell, we were in our front yard just a few feet from our front door. We might as well have been a few miles away from our house. No matter how hard he tried, Babby could not get back on his feet, and I was not strong enough to help him. I rushed into the house and called our pastor who lived nearby, praying he would be available. He came running over and helped Babby get up and into the house, even staying for a few minutes to make sure he was all right. I was deeply grateful for this angel as well.

After Babby's falls, I realized he needed attention around the clock. I wrote an email to a family friend, sharing how God was giving me the strength to take care of Babby at home, although it was getting harder. My friend wrote in reply, "I know God will give you what you need, when you need it, but I also believe that it may come from the help of others as well. I know from personal experience of helping with all four of my grandparents, that taking care of someone can be exhausting." He suggested that there may come a time when I needed to hire someone to help Babby at home. He recommended a man who had worked at the local nursing home and had come by his grandfather's house every morning to help him shave, shower and get dressed. "Granddaddy loved him," he wrote.

This information was encouraging to me. Previously I had wondered who in the world might be able and willing to help with such personal matters. I knew the time had come to seek in-home help for Babby when it became more and more difficult for him to get in the tub for a shower. A fall in the bathroom could be disastrous, I realized. I called a lady at the local nursing home to inquire about the man my friend recommended. This conversation led me to Nathaniel, who was not the man my friend recommended, but was another excellent caregiver who lived in town. I had no problem getting in touch with Nathaniel. God had sent me another people-angel. Nathaniel was gentle and kind, and Babby seemed to enjoy his light-hearted banter. He came three times a week, plus he stayed with Babby when I went to choir practice on Wednesday nights.

There were other people-angels God sent or prompted. For instance, one day as I drove Babby to get a haircut, I wondered how I would be able to help him up the steep curb in front of the barbershop. Lo and behold, just as we parked, our local hometown physician — Babby's primary care doctor — walked up! He helped Babby out of the car, gave him the support he needed to get up the high curb and into the barbershop, then lingered to help him down the curb and back into the car after his haircut. What a generous gift of his time! I was also amazed and grateful for God's perfect timing, sending Babby's doctor to lend his compassionate helping hands just when needed.

I cannot believe that these and other encounters were happenstance. Surely God arranged them to help us at our points of need.

God also prompted people to minister specifically to me sometimes. For instance, one Sunday morning, my stomach didn't feel well and I couldn't get to Sunday School or church, much to my disappointment. That afternoon four friends, including our choir director, called. They were like dear people-angels to me, bringing messages of caring concern, lifting my spirits.

I can't count the number of times people shared they were praying for Babby and me, some complete strangers. I was grateful to live in a small town where people knew and cared about each other. It always touched me deeply whenever people told me they were praying for us. They were like God's ministering angels.

13

NEARING THE END

Babby's health started going downhill faster after he had a small stroke at the end of April, 2009. Until then he had been able to walk the three blocks to Tank & Tummy for breakfast, then walk back home.

As I've noted before, the fellowship with the men at the restaurant was as good for him as the food. It was good for me, too, giving me some quiet time at home with the Lord in prayer and in the Bible as I drank a cup of tea in the mornings.

One day after Babby returned home from breakfast I saw him shuffling through the house, leaning precariously to his right side. His odd gait hindered his balance and he nearly fell several times. The leaning continued even when he sat down in his chair. I knew something was wrong and he needed to see his doctor right away. While he didn't object to going to see the doctor, his body and mind seemed confused about how to go about doing that. With some difficulty I managed to get him into the car and took him to his doctor's office about three blocks away. But there was not a single parking place anywhere near the office. I knew he would not be able to walk more than a few feet to the door, even if he leaned on me. And if he fell . . . I didn't want to think about that. So I took him to the fire department a few blocks away and asked them to check his blood pressure as he sat in the car. It was in the normal range — nothing to be alarmed about. Then I drove him home and called the doctor's office, explaining the situation. I was told to bring him to the office the next morning. Calling in the reserves, I phoned and emailed several people asking for prayer.

 When we saw his doctor the next day, he said he thought Babby probably did have a mild stroke and ordered a CT scan that day to see if there was any bleeding on his brain. Thank God no bleeding was detected. The doctor also ordered an MRI to determine the extent of the damage, but the earliest that could be scheduled was two days later.

I could hardly believe that in two days he was physically considerably better! No longer was he leaning like a half-blown-over light pole. He was still somewhat weak, and the stroke apparently had eroded more of his comprehension, making it hard for him to understand much of what I said.

The MRI results were troubling. The worst part showed how much his brain had constricted and decreased in size. Due to the effects of vascular dementia, his brain had literally shrunk. *It's a wonder he can do anything,* I sighed. And grieved. And worried. And prayed pleading prayers on my knees.

The following Sunday morning, with the warm spring sun smiling on us through the greening trees, Babby and I slowly walked to church holding hands as a mockingbird joyously sang out to the neighborhood. I was glad we went to church. The message of the sermon seemed to be meant for me. The lay speaker spoke about seasons of change being as inevitable as death and taxes, and how Jesus wants to change us and help us deal with changes that come into our lives. I knew Babby faced inevitable deteriorating changes, and I was going to need God's help all the more as Babby depended on me more and more. One saving grace was Babby's gratitude for all I did for him, from helping him get dressed to fixing his breakfast or re-tying his errant shoelace. "I don't know what I'd do without you," he would say.

I updated family and friends about his condition, asking for continued prayer. "Please ask God to protect Babby from another stroke that would be disabling. With his vascular dementia, strokes are a continual risk factor," I emailed a friend. "I can't stand the thought of his being paralyzed in a nursing home. I'm asking our Lord to protect him from a bad stroke until it's time for him to go to heaven. Thanks for your previous prayers for both of us," I added, "especially the one asking God to help me rest in Jesus' promise that we are in His hand, and 'no power can shake us out.'"

I hung onto another Bible promise, as things got more and more difficult, discovering that day by day God's grace is indeed sufficient for me no matter what. Jesus Himself said, "My power is made perfect in weakness."[1] Thank God for that! Still, I wondered and worried and prayed, reaching out to God for help and hope again and again.

JOANNE HAND

Joanne & Babby; November 2008

14

God's Grace in Dementia

How did God enable me to take care of my husband at home through his four or five years of dementia without both of us losing hope or going crazy? Three words point to the answer: God's amazing grace!

Throughout those years, no matter how much we struggled to get through each day, no matter how much I plowed through weariness and worry, the Lord always provided grace notes to soothe, strengthen, and carry both me and Babby in spite of the struggles.

Sometimes those grace notes were gifts of words when I listened intently to Him during my times of prayer and journaling. Other times those grace notes were wondrous small miracles.

Consider an entry in my prayer journal on May 5, 2009, at 2:40 a.m., a few months before the end of our dementia journey when Babby went to be with the Lord.

> *"Lord, protect me from the evil one! Give me Your peace, Lord Jesus. And Lord, You know I need to sleep. Dear Lord, it's the middle of the night. I woke up with a nightmare and my heart pounding. You know my fears about Babby having another stroke, a disabling one. So I put my fears about him and about me in Your hands as I release us into Your care. Help us, hold us close to You!*
>
> *Now help me to listen to You, Holy Spirit."*

The following is what I heard His Spirit softly tell me in my mind as I wrote in my journal. Much of it echoed Scripture; God's words of hope and peace, love and assurance spoken to me personally:

> *"Be still and know I am God.[1] Peace, be still. Peace I give unto you, Joanne, not as the world gives, but as I give. Let your heart be not troubled or afraid.[2] Remember how much I love you both.*
>
> *These waters—these troubles—will not overwhelm you[3] because I am carrying you. I will sustain you,*

and I will rescue you.[4] *Remember I hold you by my hand. Do not be afraid, for I am with you. I will strengthen you. I will help you, (and Babby too). I will uphold you in my victorious right hand.*[5]

Remember I, your God, work all things for good for those who love Me,[6] *even your frightened, pounding heart. Even Babby's dementia. As a mother comforts her child, so I will comfort you.*[7] *Lean into my embrace. I will never let you go. I will never fail you or forsake you.*[8]

Trust in the Lord with all your heart. (Help me, Lord!) Lean not unto your own understanding. Acknowledge Me in all your ways. And I will direct your steps.[9]

And now go back to bed. Even if you cannot go back to sleep, know I will sustain you in My strength. Choose to believe that My grace is sufficient for you, for My power is perfected in your weakness.[10] *And cast all your fears upon Me.*[11] *Let Me handle them—you certainly can't. Trust Me to take care of you and Babby according to My purpose and plan. And remember I am with you always.*[12] *Lean into My embrace. My everlasting arms are underneath you.*[13] *Even youths grow weary. But they who wait upon the Lord—look for, expect and hope in the Lord—will renew their strength."*[14]

I went back to bed and I did sleep, about five hours altogether, thank the Lord!

Grace notes also flowed through Babby sometimes. I remember how Babby prayed for me on one occasion when I was feeling sick, not long after my late night journaling experience. He prayed a wonderfully coherent prayer, straight from the heart of Jesus, I'm sure. It was like God holding us both, comforting us both. The Holy Spirit must have bypassed his damaged mind and prayed directly through Babby's soul which was, and is, eternally in union with the Lord regardless of the disconnected state of his mind.

This reassures me that Jesus never forgets us, never forsakes us and constantly redeems our worst experiences, even when disease steals memories and words, and fatigue steals strength! My experience shows that God's prayers of comfort reach beyond diseased minds and renew worn-out bodies. Thanks be to God for His caring, wondrous, small miracles of sustaining grace!

Sometimes, though, His grace seemed to hide out of sight. One day I wrote in my prayer journal, *"Oh Lord, lift Babby's spirits. He looks so sad! This morning he kept saying, 'What a mess! I don't know what to do.' Lift him up on eagles' wings. Fill his heart once more with Your love, Lord. Fill him up to overflowing!"* I begged God to help him. It nearly broke my heart to see my husband so depressed, either as a result of his dementia, or in addition to it.

After Babby's breakfast that morning, I led him in some exercises which seemed to help. I also asked his doctor about increasing Babby's antidepressant. The doctor agreed it might make a difference. After a time, that seemed to ease Babby's sadness, thank the Lord! The medications prescribed for him in the early days of his disease helped him for many months. Of course there was no cure, but I was grateful for anything that restored even a small measure of mental clarity and reduced his confusion. Over a period of a few years, however, the disease gradually overwhelmed what the medicine could do.

Sometimes I wondered if fatigue would overwhelm me. Nevertheless, God gave me the strength to keep going by waking me up early each morning so I could meet with Him for my daily devotional time before Babby woke up. I was amazed how the Holy Spirit often directed me to Scripture passages that spoke directly to my need for that day, reassuring me, comforting me, lifting my spirits, and drawing me closer as I leaned on Him. I knew His strength would sustain me because that's what He promised. It meant everything to me to pour out my heart, my fears, and my frustrations to the Lord, knowing He listened compassionately. What's more, when I asked the Holy Spirit to help me listen to Him, He did. His answers always filled me with quiet, sustaining joy.

These talks with the Lord especially helped me when communicating with Babby became very challenging. The last few months of his life, Babby could hardly understand anything I said. It was as if I was speaking a foreign language to him. He gave me the most baffled look, no matter how simply I tried to explain something. So we ate in silence or listened to music while we ate without talking. For someone like me who loves to talk (sometimes too much!), that was sad. The silence weighed on my heart.

But I could still talk with the Lord anytime throughout the day. I knew He was always with me and Babby, as close as a prayer. The hymn "What a Friend We Have in Jesus" by Joseph Medlicott Scriven, described how I felt. The first part of the third verse spoke strongest to me:

> "Are we weak and heavy laden,
> cumbered with a load of care?
> Precious Savior, still our refuge,
> take it to the Lord in prayer."[15]

I'm also deeply grateful that I could talk with a few close friends and our two sons. Thank God for telephones and email!

The latter part of May 2009, about four months before Babby died, a problem loomed larger than a mountain — one I didn't think I could climb. Babby began sleeping until 9:00 a.m. or later every morning. I wondered how I could get us to our Sunday School class and church on time. Trying to wake Babby up and get him going was like trying to wake up an immovable rock. There seemed to be no way I could get him to take his pills, help him get dressed (which was a difficult process and took quite a while), fix his breakfast, get myself ready, and get us to Sunday School by 10:00 a.m. The caregiver who came three days a week to help Babby shave and get dressed couldn't come on Sundays.

I also wondered how I could find time to prepare to teach the Sunday School lesson every other Sunday. I enjoyed teaching, and learned much more by studying to teach than just reading the lesson. Also, the fellowship of discussing the lesson during our class was meaningful to me. Furthermore, it was such a joy to sing to God with the choir at church, and to listen to His messages in the music and the sermons. *Would I have to give all this up?* I wondered.

But lo and behold, when Sunday mornings rolled around, Babby got up around 7:00 a.m., giving us plenty of time to get ready and arrive early to Sunday School! I could almost hear the Lord saying, *See, silly one, I will work out whatever I need you to do. Why did you think I wouldn't? Oh ye of little faith! I will always make a way for you to adequately prepare to teach when you need to teach.*

It had never occurred to me to ask God to work it out. I just sadly assumed that I would have to give up Sunday School and church as Babby got worse and worse. But God had other grace notes planned as we faced more struggles.

15

Falling in Love with a Pilot

"Would you believe we've been married fifty years today?" I asked Babby, noting the date on the calendar, June 18, 2009. Babby half smiled, not understanding. "We got married June 18, 1959, at the Methodist Church in Florence, Alabama," I reminded him.

Memories flooded my mind, making me smile. I'll never forget the day I first met Babby about two years before we married. It was a placid spring Sunday morning in Florence and I was running a bit late for church. I quietly rushed into my Sunday School class for college students. Settling down and catching my breath, I noticed a good-looking guy I'd not seen before. Turns out, he was considerably older than my freshmen friends who attended the local college, including me. He had already graduated from Georgia Tech and spent two years in the Air Force. At the time I met him he had just started working at the Tennessee Valley Authority near Florence as a chemical engineer. I also learned his nickname was "Babby," short for Larrabee. Until then, I'd never heard either name before. I liked the sound of it and it seemed to match his boyish grin. This was Babby's first visit to our church, and since there wasn't a young adult class he could attend, he was directed to the college class. Suited him fine, he told me later with a shy grin, since he came hoping to meet some "young ladies."

After Sunday School was dismissed, I overheard that Babby owned a small two-seater airplane. I thought, *Oh, wow!* Striking up a conversation with the charming aviator a little later, I welcomed him to Florence, introduced myself and then lost no time telling him I had never flown before, but that I really would like to! He took the bait! (Or was the airplane the bait, and I swallowed it? Wings, propeller, pilot and all!) In any case, after the church service, Babby asked me if I would like to go flying with him that night. I jumped at the chance. But there was just one catch. Since I was eighteen and still living at home with my parents, I would need to get my father's permission. I invited my newfound dashing friend to drive me home so he could meet my parents, and I could get the green light to go flying with him. When we walked into the living room, my mother was in the kitchen, and my dad was in the bedroom taking a nap. Telling my mom what I hoped to do, she said, "Ask your dad," adding she didn't think he was asleep since he had just laid down a couple of minutes earlier.

Taking a deep breath as I entered the bedroom, I nervously presented my request. "Daddy, I've met this really nice guy in Sunday School, and he owns a small airplane. He asked me to go flying with him tonight. I asked Mom, but she said to ask you."

Daddy sat up and said in a gruff voice, "What do you mean, go flying with some guy you just met? What do you know about him? How well does he know how to fly?"

My heart sank. What if he refused to let me go? "But Daddy," I said, recovering my resolve as I remembered what I had learned about this pilot. "He has been in the Air Force. Don't you think serving in the Air Force for two years would make him a good pilot?"

What I did not tell my dad was the fact that Babby had not flown in the Air Force. He joined the Air Force hoping to fly, but a few years earlier a serious motorcycle accident had left him unconscious in the hospital — in a coma — for several days, disqualifying him from the highly competitive flight training. However, Babby did take private flying lessons during his time off while in the Air Force. I didn't tell my dad those details, counting on the Air Force credentials alone to persuade him. It worked! My dad reluctantly agreed to let me go fly with him in his airplane.

At the airport, Babby pulled his silver Ercoupe out of the hangar, then carefully checked every part of the plane. But when we climbed into the small cockpit, he had second thoughts about flying that night. The weather wasn't a concern because a gorgeous full moon shimmered in the clear night sky, perfect for flying, it seemed to me. I don't know why he decided it wouldn't be wise to fly that night. It didn't matter. We sat in the cockpit and talked and talked, getting to know each other. What impressed me was the way he didn't take advantage of the romantic setting, not even lightly putting his arm around my shoulder. I felt comfortable with this new friend, safe, and intrigued. He promised he would take me flying in the daytime, the following Saturday, weather permitting. Before long we went flying almost every weekend. I loved the adventure of flying, and I soon fell in love with the pilot.

Why did I love him? It did my heart good to count the ways, paraphrasing the poet Elizabeth Barrett Browning in her famous "Sonnet 43."[1] He was gentle and kind, not just to me, but also to children, dogs and cats. Whenever he came upon a dog or cat, he stooped to pet it. Whenever he saw a child, he'd break out in a big smile. He enjoyed his sisters' young children when we flew over to visit them near Atlanta. That told me he would make a good dad. As it turned out, I was right, twice over. I couldn't ask for a better father for our two sons. That included changing diapers, getting up for midnight bottle feedings, and playing piggyback when they were old enough to sit up and hang on. He loved spending time with them, and there wasn't anything he wouldn't do for them.

Beyond that, I loved his core-deep honesty and integrity, his quiet humbleness, his servant's heart, and his generous, giving nature. Sometimes I thought he was too generous for his own good, but I had to remind myself that was part of why I loved him.

One of his most endearing characteristics was his wacky sense of humor. He kept me laughing, right up to the last month of his life, even with full-blown dementia.

Remarkably, by the grace of God, his dementia did not steal one iota of any of these characteristics. His brain could no longer calculate numerical equations in a flash or handle our finances like before, but he still gave me hugs occasionally. Even though his words were few and broken as his cognitive abilities began to deteriorate, I remembered the early days of his dementia when he told me he loved me far more often than before. That memory always touched my heart. It still does.

Still, it saddened me that he couldn't remember how we met more than 50 years earlier, or our wedding, or our honeymoon in Bermuda. On the way to Bermuda we spent the night in New York City and saw *My Fair Lady* on Broadway. On the way home to Alabama we spent the night in Washington, D.C. and saw a comedy on stage called, *Harvey*. Those wonderful memories shine in my mind as clearly as if they happened last week, but he couldn't remember them at all, even when I fondly related them to him.

God must have seen my sadness because he blessed me with a devotional that showed up in my email inbox on our wedding anniversary in 2009. The devotional, called "Promise Kept," highlighted a couple's 50th wedding anniversary, looking at how God keeps his loving promises to us forever. I felt as if God reached down and touched me, saying, "See, I remember! And My love for you both has been overflowing your hearts all these years, and will continue forever." Only God could arrange that particular devotional to show up as an email on our own 50th anniversary. I needed that reminder of what's most important.

As the Bible says, "Love is patient, love is kind…bears all things, believes all things, hopes all things, endures all things. Love never fails."[2]

Even when my love is not patient or kind, or stumbles through bearing, believing, and enduring; even when our minds fail, God's love never fails, and lasts forever. "Underneath are the everlasting arms,"[3] as God's Word also promises. All that comforted me, and sustained me further.

This was reinforced on our 50th wedding anniversary when I happened to see a video of our church's Valentine's Day service on the internet. Ben, our music director, contrasted the way our culture views love as overpowering, whereas Scripture views love as empowering. I needed that contrasting reminder. Looking back, I could see that

God had kept me going through His empowering, unfailing love for Babby and me, and through our love for each other for more than fifty years, in spite of our failures and weaknesses, in spite of dementia. Thanks be to God!

To celebrate the day with food, I drove to the local restaurant downtown called Grandma's Table, a favorite for traditional cooked-from-scratch Southern cuisine, bringing home two take-outs. It was a lovely meal, more than we could eat, seasoned with gratitude.

Babby as a boy (circa 1939). Perhaps the flying goggles – probably borrowed from his father who owned and flew an open cockpit biplane for a short time — inspired him to become a pilot.

Babby & Joanne's wedding day in 1959.

16
Wrestling Through the 23rd Psalm

"*Oh Lord, don't let him have cancer! Not on top of dementia! Once again I'm floundering in the 'what ifs.' Lord, give me your strength and peace!*" I wrote in my prayer journal.

I was struggling with fear facing my husband's signs of possible colon cancer. The symptoms were small at first, and they came and went like my worries. When the symptoms worsened, questions haunted me: *Would I need to put him through grueling tests? Would he need surgery?* Over and over I begged God to heal him of whatever was causing the problem.

I wrestled with the "what ifs" for weeks before I could get a doctor's appointment. Finally, God used the 23rd Psalm to calm me down one pre-dawn morning. He walked me through the psalm like a reassuring two-way prayer.

"The Lord is my shepherd. I shall not want."[1]

But I do want and need much, Lord. I need Your guidance and strength. I need Your help and healing for Babby.

"He maketh me to lie down in green pastures. He leadeth me beside the still waters. He restoreth my soul: he leadeth me in the paths of righteousness for his name's sake."[2]

But how, Lord? I hoped for practical examples.

"Be still and know I am God,"[3] He answered in my mind. And listen.

After listening in my mind and heart for a while, I sensed the Lord was inviting me to get out of bed every morning before Babby woke up, and meet our Lord for a devotional date. Until that time I had let fatigue keep me in bed until I had to help Babby get up, give him his pills, and fix breakfast. (This was when Babby was no longer able to walk to Tank and Tummy for breakfast.) But a date with my

Lord? That sounded exciting, but hard. *Oh Lord, I'd love to, but You will have to wake me up early enough, and give me the strength to get up.* To my surprise, He did! Every morning the joy of the Lord woke me up and helped me crawl out of bed, fighting fatigue. *Perk me up, please,* I frequently prayed. *Help me to listen to You. And thank You for letting Babby sleep late.*

It was amazing how often God gave me spiritual hugs of encouragement as I drank deeply from his Word. Similarly, short stories of faith from *The Upper Room* devotional magazine, which I read daily, seemed to come straight from God's heart just for me, restoring my fearful soul at least for that day. Furthermore, God continued to provide care for Babby at home while I escaped to choir rehearsal for two hours every Wednesday night. That gave me refreshing "green pasture" times as we rehearsed Scripture-based songs and hymns. Our choir director always led us in brief discussions about the meaning of the Scripture underlying our music, and how the lyrics of the songs related to the Scripture and to us personally. This added the more fortifying soul food I needed to give me energy and peace for each day.

God also answered my prayer by enabling Babby and me to get to Sunday School before the church service, even though getting ready was no easy task. The fellowship with class members, and enlightening discussions about the Scripture lessons blessed me, making the difficult effort to get to the class well worth it. Because of Babby's wobbling walking gait, we usually walked the two blocks from our house to the Sunday School class tightly holding hands like sweethearts, a bonus blessing.

These refreshing, faith-strengthening times helped me trust God to lead us through dark and difficult paths. As I prayed silently, *"Yea though I walk through the valley of the shadow of death, I will fear no evil. Thy rod and thy staff they comfort me,"*[4] from the 23rd Psalm, I could see how the shepherd's rod and staff symbolized our Lord's protection and guidance. This gave me an unshakable sense of peace even in the face of possible cancer.

The resulting peace cleared the way for a decision: Babby's doctor and I decided that we would not put Babby through any difficult tests. The doctor said Babby was in an advanced stage of vascular dementia, and a stroke resulting from that disease could end his life before cancer could develop serious side effects or become life-threatening. We chose the path of benign neglect. I trusted that path to be the right one. *Thank You, Lord, for always walking with us, keeping us close to You, shepherding us day by day,* I prayed gratefully.

"You anoint my head with oil, my cup overflows,"[5] Psalm 23 continues. My Good Shepherd-Lord seemed to be saying that He would anoint my anxious mind with His caring comfort, and refill my empty cup to overflowing with His steadfast, unfailing love.

"Lord, thank You so much for breaking through my tense 'what ifs,' giving me peace and assurance," I wrote in my prayer journal. *"It is well with my soul! Praise God! I love You, Lord! If I could hug You, Lord Jesus, I would. Maybe I just did with those grateful words."*

"Surely your goodness and unfailing love will pursue me all the days of my life, and I will live in the house of the LORD forever."[6]

17

A Temporary Reprieve

One Sunday morning in August 2009, Babby suddenly could not stand up. It was as if his legs couldn't get enough of a signal from his brain to do anything other than remain locked in place. After he repeatedly tried to get up from the couch to no avail, I called 911. The ambulance took him about ten miles away to Mitchell County Hospital in Camilla as I followed in my car.

Just before we left, I had called a church friend to let her know why we wouldn't be in Sunday School or church, asking for prayers.

The word spread like wildfire, setting off prayers in all the adult Sunday School classes, and at choir practice before the worship service began. Our pastor also offered prayer for us at the beginning of the church service. We were enveloped in prayers. I could actually feel those prayers as God filled me with His peace: the peace that passes understanding, the peace of His reassuring presence. In my mind I heard Jesus tell the storm of my anxious worries, *"Peace, be still,"*[1] and to my surprise, my mental storm ceased! I knew He was with us and helping us, somehow, someway.

While we were waiting in the Emergency Room, Babby's cousin, Sue, showed up. As soon as she heard that we had gone to the hospital, she immediately left church and drove straight to the ER. Her caring presence put Babby at ease as he smiled broadly when he saw her. While we waited for a doctor, she said, "Let's have prayer together." We circled up, the two of us holding hands with Babby and with each other as he lay on the examining table. It was just what I needed, and Babby too.

God went beyond prayers in another way that amazed me. That Sunday afternoon, after Babby had been released from the ER into an open hospital room, he wanted to get out of bed and walk around. I encouraged him to try, although I doubted he would be able to walk. But he did! Holding onto my hand lightly, we walked out of the hospital room, strolled around the whole corridor, and circled the nurses' station. I felt I had witnessed a miracle, and couldn't thank God enough! No, Babby wasn't healed of dementia, but his walking ability had been restored, at least for a while.

The doctor on call said that Babby would likely have another episode worse than the first. I knew that was probably true, but I believed we had been given a reprieve. I explained that as long as he could walk, even a little in the house, I could take care of him at home. "Can we go home now?" I asked. The doctor reluctantly released him, and I drove Babby home. The next morning, as I wondered what I should do next, I called Sue for advice. She told me to try to get an appointment with Babby's primary care doctor right away, which I did. While we were waiting in the doctor's office, Sue came bearing a gift of pear muffins just out of her oven. She had been baking when I called, planning to give the muffins away to people who needed cheering up. What a delicious ministry!

The following morning I struggled again with worry and what ifs. I called another friend, asking for some extra prayer. I shared that Babby's doctor had explained the previous day that he thought Babby had experienced a transient ischemic attack (TIA), a short-lived mini-stroke, and was at high risk for a major stroke. I agreed that preparations needed to be made to move Babby into the Pelham nursing home in case he lost his mobility permanently. God gave my friend some reassuring words, just as the Holy Spirit also spoke through a few other friends. A couple of those friends talked with me via email, one referring to Scripture that comforted me. They all assured me that they were praying for us.

Our son David drove to Pelham the day after Babby's visit to the ER and stayed with us until Friday afternoon. He was a tremendous help with his dad and accompanied me to the local nursing home to talk with the director there. She was kind and helpful, and yet my heart ached. We asked several questions and learned that even though the admittance process might involve a wait of several weeks, the decision would be up to me if I needed to move Babby into nursing home care.

I was grateful that we had the best nursing home we could hope for so close to our house. Still, I could hardly bear the thought of putting Babby there. He would feel abandoned and lost. That would be heartbreaking for me. And yet, I knew I would not be strong enough to care for and assist Babby at home if he had a paralyzing stroke.

I emailed a friend asking for prayer that God would work this out according to His plan. After all, God loved Babby even more than I did. He knew what was best. "Pray for peace for us both," I asked.

In spite of my fears and fatigue, God gave me His peace once again, as He comforted me day by day, prayer by prayer, little by little.

Nevertheless, I was physically exhausted and heart-weary from constantly caring for my husband at home. Babby also struggled with exhaustion as it took all he could put forward mentally to continue to move about the house and engage in simple daily tasks. It was getting harder and harder for us both.

Even though Nathaniel, the kind man I had hired to help bathe and shave Babby, came three times a week, I carried the brunt of his everyday care as he became less and less able to do things for himself. Soon he couldn't remember how to tie his shoes. Although he continued to love to hold our dog Chance in his lap, Babby lost interest in watching TV with the dog — I assume because he couldn't make sense of anything on the screen. My heart hurt watching him deteriorate before my eyes. However, I was grateful I could still take care of him at home.

DEALING WITH DEMENTIA

My mainstay recourse was to pour out my feelings to the Lord in my prayer journal first thing in the morning before Babby got out of bed. Sometimes I wrote, *"Lord, let me listen to You now,"* then wrote down what I heard Him say in my mind.

In my prayer journal, I wrote what I believed God was saying to me:

> *"Be still and know I AM God[2] – your God, your Comforter and Shepherd and Counselor and Savior and your dearest, closest Friend. I delight in you, Joanne, and I carry you over all the rough places. My love for you (and for all My children), is undying and unfailing, unfolding forever more. Keep close to Me. Keep listening to Me in My Word and in your heart. Keep praying for others and for the church. Remember I'm praying with you and through you. Give thanks in all circumstances.[3] Keep trusting Me to work all things for good."*

> *"For it is [not your strength, but it is] God who is effectively at work in you, both to will and to work [that is, strengthening, energizing, and creating in you the longing and the ability to fulfill your purpose] for His good pleasure."*[4]

God's words poured new life, strength and encouragement into my tired body and soul. I thanked God, wanting to hug Him. Instead, I hugged Babby and told him I loved him. In the earlier stages of his disease he would frequently hug me which was such a joy. In those days we also exchanged "I love you" quite often, and that was a balm for my hurting heart. In the later stage of his disease, I clung to the memories of earlier exchanges.

In one of the most poignant later symptoms of the disease, Babby acted like he was in a strange place and expressed a bewildered desire to go home. When I reassured him that he *was* home, he seemed relieved, but then forgot and asked again to go home. He didn't get agitated about it, but it seemed to trouble him.

One of the most heartbreaking things of all was Babby's frustration at not being able to do things for himself. "Just throw me away," he'd say. Or, "Just put me some place and leave me. I don't know what to do. I can't do anything. Can you tell me what to do? All I do is sit in this (living room) chair, over and over." Our little dog snuggled beside him in the chair, offering comfort as best he could. They napped there together.

The next Sunday morning, I left Babby at home with a friend while I attended our church service. Although Babby didn't seem to understand what day it was or where I was going, attending church without my husband was hard. For years we had walked, holding hands, down the block and around the corner to the church entrance. Walking alone felt weary and lonely. Following lunch, I emailed several friends an update about how Babby and I were doing. Just sharing my own troubled feelings washed away my weariness, at least for a while. In one of those emails I wrote, "I'm so thankful God made a way for me to come to worship this morning and sing to the Lord with the choir. I desperately needed it. The organ and piano music, as well as Pastor Michael's sermon, and Communion all fed and lifted my soul. The postlude on the organ gave me a comforting image of the Lord holding me in His strong arms and *dancing* with me! That makes me smile just to think about it. That's the joy of the Lord for sure! I'm hanging onto that as I let Him hold onto me. He's holding Babby, too, I'm sure. It just occurred to me I need to pray for the peace that Jesus gives, the peace that passes understanding, for Babby. I've asked for peace for myself many times, and He always gives it to me, but I hadn't thought to ask for it for Babby."

Asking for prayer also helped me. In another email to a different friend on August 31, 2009, I wrote, "This morning Babby had another TIA (a small temporary stroke). I called Nathaniel — our caregiver — and he helped me take Babby to the doctor's office. The doctor said that Babby will keep on having these episodes. When the next one happens, the doctor told me to call 911 and get the ambulance to take him to the hospital. In the meantime, we're working to get him into the nursing home here when a bed opens up. Please pray that this works out according to God's plan. Pray for peace for Babby and for me, and strength and steadiness for me."

I knew I couldn't take care of Babby if he couldn't walk, and his legs were getting weaker and wobblier. Of course putting him in a nursing home wouldn't be easy, but God was easing my heart towards that solution. As it turned out, the nursing home was not in God's plan. God's plan was much harder, yet in the end, much better.

18

Peace in the Final Days

Even through the nightmare of my husband's last days on earth, God's intervening grace comforted and sustained me. That is, for a while. Then, for a time, nothing seemed to help.

Most of the time God's grace flowed through people who responded to my prayer request emails or talked with me on the phone. Even as hopeless as those days were, people expressing compassion and promising to pray for us encouraged and strengthened me. Babby was on a downward spiral, in his final days of struggle with vascular dementia.

I don't know how I would have coped without talking about his struggles and mine with our two sons and a few friends. Knowing they cared for us and were praying for us lifted my sagging spirits.

For example, I emailed a friend the following message: "This afternoon Babby started to hit me as I was trying to help him. He didn't want to be bothered, but I needed to change his clothes. He was so tired, he just wanted me to leave him alone, but I couldn't because he was wet. When he balled up his fist to hit me, I screamed and started to cry. That scared him, and then he realized what he had almost done, and he was sorry. I know it was the disease that made him act that way, but it shook me up. Please pray that God will restore his gentle spirit. Thanks for lifting us up in prayer," I concluded.

Two days later I emailed another friend. "Babby has turned terribly hostile and uncooperative. He's still in bed — although it is almost 1:00 in the afternoon. He got up briefly to go to the bathroom, but when I asked him if I could help him, he snarled at me to get out, and went back to bed. Several times I gently urged him to get up, rubbed his back, kissed him on the cheek, but the last time I got near him, he tried to hit me. He did that once yesterday, but then turned sweet again, and I thought God had answered my prayer to restore his sweet spirit. I've called the doctor, and I am waiting for a call back. Babby hasn't had his pills, nor anything to drink or eat today. He might be dehydrated. My heart is sick, as you can imagine. Part of me wishes that the doctor would just call to reassure me that it's alright to call 911 and get him on the path to the nursing home. Better still, I pray God will restore Babby to his right spirit, if not his right mind."

As I added in my email, Babby's doctor had told me earlier that if — or rather, *when* — Babby got to the point where he couldn't walk or became disabled in another way, I should call 911 and allow him to be admitted to the hospital. The staff could treat him as best they could, but mainly get him on track for the local nursing home as soon as a bed opened up.

Finally the doctor called me back and told me to go ahead and dial 911. By the grace of God, Babby turned gentle and cooperative, allowing me to change his clothes before the ambulance arrived. Although he went willingly, he could not walk, so they had to carry him on a stretcher.

The initial tests at the hospital were briefly agonizing. "Get me out of here," Babby begged, pleading with me to take him home. I had to steel my heart, explaining that we had to see if they could help him. I don't think he understood, but he didn't ask again. The nurses took his vital signs and checked for obvious symptoms of a stroke. Every time they would touch him, Babby would hiss through his teeth or groan. I hated it. At the same time I was grateful he wasn't lashing out angrily, or balling up his fist the way he had earlier. He felt so miserable and weak. He just wanted to be left alone. Although I realized that, it still hurt and haunted me. Finally Babby was admitted to a room where he could rest. He was exhausted, and I was too. But, by the grace of God, he seemed to be at peace, no longer apprehensive about staying at the hospital.

Tests at the hospital revealed he had a bladder infection. Within just a few hours of antibiotic treatment, his condition noticeably improved and Babby seemed in better spirits. Did I dare hope again?

A couple of days later, as Babby remained at the hospital, continuing antibiotic treatment, another setback occurred. I sent out an email SOS prayer request. "Babby needs lots of extra prayer. After doing amazingly well yesterday, he's had a big setback today. He's not able to swallow this afternoon and evening, and he's vomiting up stuff like dark red blood this morning. He's on IV fluids and is sleeping with his mouth open. He's also flushed and hot on his face. He seems pretty miserable–obviously feeling bad. My heart breaks to watch him."

I called our son David and asked him to come back. He had come earlier when his father was taken to the hospital, but returned home when he improved. As I told my friend, "I'm thankful that David can stay with me at least until this gets resolved." I didn't realize until later that Babby had suffered a stroke which impeded his swallowing. Regardless, I felt certain he was headed for the nursing home. I accepted that, but my heart was doubly heavy with dread, helplessly watching him suffer. We both desperately needed God's comforting embrace, but I felt forsaken. Was this how Jesus felt on the cross?

19

Alligator Goodbye

I needed comfort, some sign of comfort to ease this heartbreaking burden. When I walked into his hospital room on Sunday morning, it seemed Babby was a little more stable and feeling somewhat better. I felt free to go to church, leaving him in the care of the nurses for a few hours. I went hoping for some scrap of reassurance that God would carry us through these worst of days. When our pastor made his usual altar call before the last hymn, I knew I had to go to the altar. Every Sunday our pastor invited the congregation to come to the altar and pray on our knees for whatever burdens we wanted to give to the Lord.

As the hymn began, I knelt at the altar with my hands extended, indicating I wanted the pastor to pray with me. Instead of taking my hands, as I thought he might, he wrapped his arms around me and asked how he could pray for me. I replied, "However you are led. I just need extra prayer." His prayer seemed to come straight from the heart of God because it was exactly the comfort I needed. The long, deep sleeves of the pastor's robe wrapped around me and gave me the sense of being held, enfolded in the wings of a comforting angel sent by God. Needless to say, I was deeply moved, almost to tears.

God's comforting hugs were repeated in several ways through different people, at the exact moments when I needed them most, especially during the last heartrending days of Babby's life. Surprisingly, God's comfort also came through Babby's expression of unexpected humor. It happened in the hospital a few days before he died. He was weak after the painful initial tests, but he wasn't begging to go home any more. I stayed with him until shortly after sunset. When I told him I was going home and would be back in the morning, I added, "I'll see you later." Quick as a flash, he replied with a weak grin, "Alligator!" The expression, "See ya later, alligator!" had been an occasional quip that Babby used to call out to me when he was leaving the house. It never failed to make me laugh.

"Alligator" was the last word he was able to say. Later I remembered his doctor had told me that a sense of humor is the last thing a dementia patient loses even after the mind and body have slid into shambles. Babby always had a wonderful wacky sense of humor, one of the endearing things I loved about him. As strange as it sounds, I'll always be grateful that the last thing he said to me was "alligator." It makes me smile every time I think about it. Yes, I cherish the many times throughout his dementia journey when he told me, "I love you," often accompanied by a hug. But it's that last wacky "alligator" goodbye that lifts my spirits the most.

After that last word, however, his suffering worsened. And yet, even those difficult days were not without a few poignant grace notes of comfort. He even seemed to improve a little in some respects, raising my hopes again for an extension of time.

"Thank You, Lord, for Babby's progress," I wrote in my prayer journal Sept. 25, 2009, two days before

he died. *"He's off the IV fluids now. Thank You most of all for restoring his sweet spirit and grateful heart."*

His swallowing improved somewhat, although he was not eating enough to keep a bird alive. Small cups of ice cream every now and then kept body and soul together. Even while dying, he still loved ice cream!

I badly needed a break from sitting in the hospital. Babby might survive for a while, but he would never recover except in heaven.

Even as I admitted my need for a break, I felt guilty. Surely I should stay by his side no matter what. Babby had been in the hospital less than a week, yet it felt like an endless desert of days.

"Oh Lord, I'm so sleepy I can hardly see straight! Should I go home and take a nap?" I wrote in my prayer journal. *"Babby is mostly sleeping. He's breathing heavy and jerking some in his sleep, his mouth open more than yesterday."* (Later I learned that his jerking was a sign that he was not getting enough oxygen to his lungs and brain.)

"Lord, it's so hard seeing him struggle!" I cried out.

That afternoon I learned he had developed pneumonia. He was put on three IV antibiotics and fluids. *Oh Lord, help him to rest easy,* I prayed. *If it's time for him to go to You in heaven, please let him slip away without any struggle. Don't let him struggle on and on!*

I told the nurse that if he stopped breathing not to take any drastic measures to resuscitate him. I prefaced that by saying, "I hope you don't think I'm strange . . . " She replied, "I don't think you're strange at all. His doctor has those instructions on his chart and I understand."

"I don't want to lose him before I have to," I explained. "But I don't want him to suffer any more than he has to, either. I've already released him to God." I added, my voice breaking a little.

"Let me give you a hug," she said, wrapping me in her arms. "I know that's a hard decision to make. Some people want to cling to their loved ones, and that's understandable. But I wouldn't want that for myself."

"And neither would I," I agreed. No doubt her hug and kind words echoed God's heart, and I clung to them. *Have mercy on him, most merciful Father,* I silently prayed for the umpteenth time.

20

The Musical Ice Cream Truck

"Mom, Daddy is breathing real slow. I think you'd better come," our son David told me when he called from the hospital.

"I'll be right there," I said. I had just crawled into bed at home to take a nap before we began a likely night-long vigil at the hospital. I needed all the strength I could get. Babby had been in an agitated semi-conscious state, apparently in a good bit of discomfort, following his most recent stroke which had made it difficult for him to swallow. I was heartbroken. I had been by his side for many days, holding his hand, silently praying for him.

After David had arrived, we took turns staying by Babby's side at the hospital. Babby had developed pneumonia, but his doctor said that since he had never smoked and he regularly enjoyed walking all over our small town, his heart and lungs were strong. In his younger days he jogged six miles several days a week and ran in races. The doctor on call that day noted that, cardiovascularly, his condition seemed fair — even considering the pneumonia. If Babby recovered, he would have to go to the local nursing home. All I could do was put him in God's hands. *Please help him, Lord! Don't let him suffer too long. Have mercy on him, most merciful Father!* After a while, my strength seemed to drain out of me. That's when I went home to take a nap, leaving David to stay with his dad for a while.

As soon as I had gotten home and laid down for a nap, David telephoned me, urging me to come back to the hospital. I ran to the car and raced through the 10 minute drive on a back road. The warm September sun was setting, shining intensely over the tree-lined horizon. "Please, Lord, let me get there in time," I implored out loud. I didn't want him to die without me at his side.

As I drove toward the hospital I saw a car to my right pulling out of a driveway headed for the two-lane road directly in front of me. *Surely, the driver will see me and stop*, I thought. But the car kept coming. Apparently the bright sun setting directly across the road blinded the driver. I jerked the wheel and swerved off the road onto the narrow shoulder to avoid a collision, throwing up a panicked prayer, *Oh Lord, don't let our sons lose both their parents on the same day!* My car rolled to a stop upright without hitting anything. I'm not sure what the other car did. I didn't wait to find out, but pulled back onto the road as quickly as I could, trembling and thanking God for protecting me from a wreck.

At the hospital I hurried up the stairs to the second floor, then flung open the door of Babby's room. David was waiting for me, standing alone, looking lost. "He's gone," he said.

We cried as we clung to each other. "I wanted so much to be with him, to hold his hand when he died!" I sobbed, telling David I wondered if his dad thought I had abandoned him. But David assured me that most importantly he had peacefully slipped away to be with the Lord, with no struggle or signs of pain. His breathing simply slowed to a stop.

David explained, "I stood close to Dad, gripping his hand, sometimes holding his arm or his head, reassuring him that I was with him and Mom was on her way. His breathing just kept getting more and more shallow. He never regained consciousness, but I have to believe he heard everything I told him. I told Dad that Jesus was waiting for him with a big smile, and it was all right to go to Jesus."

Hearing that comforted me more than I could say. I also was comforted remembering that David and I both had told him repeatedly in those last hours that we loved him.

Our other son, Hollis, also had assured his dad he loved him on the telephone from his home in North Carolina. Hollis had called several times to talk to me and his dad those last few days at the hospital. Although Babby could not talk back, he listened while David and I held the phone as Hollis spoke. Earlier that day, Hollis and his wife Sheila had felt it was time to join us at the hospital and had started the long drive down to Mitchell County. They arrived less than two hours after Babby died. Babby had slipped away quicker than I had thought he might, but thankfully without a prolonged struggle, and in God's perfect timing, as we explained to Hollis and Sheila.

After we all talked quietly for a while in the hospital room, grappling with our emotions, two of

Babby's nurses came in, one at a time. They embraced me and let me cry on their shoulders. Both times I felt God holding me close. That was the beginning of several heartfelt and comforting hugs from many people.

There were other ways God comforted me. These included the funeral service at our church when we celebrated Babby's life on earth and his new life in heaven fully restored in every way. Surely he was praising God in the company of a jubilant cloud of witnesses, inviting us to join their songs of wondrous thanksgiving.

The most unforgettable comfort came in the guise of a musical ice cream truck at the graveside service following the funeral at our church. The brief service was held at the old Pelham Cemetery under a tall outreaching magnolia tree. Many other stately trees arched towards the sky and enveloped the entire cemetery and neighborhood. The Georgia pines with their unique but unmistakable soft trill in the wind gently whistled.

Soon after the service began, a musical ice cream truck stopped on the side of the road outside the iron fence that surrounded the cemetery, parking several yards from where our family gathered. When I heard the small truck playing inviting music, I couldn't help but smile thinking how much Babby loved ice cream. Grateful for the lilting music, I hardly noticed that the truck played one song over and over throughout the duration of the funeral service. Gradually the joyful, uplifting tune seeped into my grieving heart like a balm. I had dreaded the funeral, but the music dissolved that dread, replacing it with reassurance.

Even though the tune of the repeated song sounded familiar, my mind hadn't thought about it long enough to recall the name of the song. After we got home I realized the full significance of the tune when Sheila pointed out that the ice cream truck had been playing, most appropriately, "When the Saints Go Marching In."[1] What an amazing send-off with words and music of God's grace! Babby loved that song, as I do, and we always would pat our feet to its rousing beat whenever we heard it, smiling broadly. What a lovely musical benediction! And what a wondrous, loving God who arranged that tailor-made ice cream song at the very time I needed it most. No doubt Jesus was grinning too, and maybe even tapping His foot!

Months later, I realized that I never saw or heard the ice cream truck in our town after that time, even during the summer of the following year. It just seemed to disappear, its sweet mission completed.

21

Comfort from Heaven

What a contrast! Soon after the funeral, I spent five comforting, delightful days with my son and his family, including my three grandchildren, who lived near Orlando in central Florida. But the delight turned into dread as my son David drove me back home to Pelham in south Georgia. Like a somber drumbeat throughout the trip, all I could think about was David having to return to Florida, leaving me alone in the house.

My dear husband had died almost two weeks earlier. The thought of living alone without him after more than fifty years of marriage made me feel empty and lost.

Many people expressed their gracious sympathy to me and cared for me during those next weeks. Some of my friends from church and former co-workers reached out to me often. A few of them deeply understood what I was going through since they had recently lost loved ones. I felt such a wellspring of gratitude for all the prayers and love that surrounded me and lifted me up after Babby's death. These were expressed in many kind words, cards, calls, visits, hugs, food and flourishing plants.

But the reality of being alone without Babby now stared me in the face like a cold monument. How would I cope?

I'll be your husband and I'll take care of you.

Those words broke into my troubled thoughts as clearly as if they had been spoken out loud. *How can that be?* I asked silently, even as comforting reassurance rushed into my heart. I didn't understand what it meant, but I knew that the Lord had spoken to me with an incredible promise. Surely I heard echoes of Scripture in those words. At home, I searched and found the reference in Isaiah 54:

> "Do not be afraid . . . For your Maker is your husband, the Lord Almighty is his name, the

Holy One of Israel is your Redeemer; he is called the God of all the earth. . . . Though the mountains be shaken and the hills be removed, yet my unfailing love for you will not be shaken nor my covenant of peace be removed, says the Lord who has compassion on you."[1]

What an amazing, mind-boggling promise! The mighty Creator of the Universe, the Father of our Lord Jesus Christ, reaching out in enduring, transforming loving-kindness to me! What a precious gift that never fades, never fails, never dies!

Strange as it may sound, even as a widow, I'll always feel married to Babby. Yet I know the Lord is my Husband now and forever. He's also my Deliverer, Savior, Comforter, Provider, Helper, Guide, and dearest, closest Friend. His peace and love hold me close. What more could I ask? Still, God showers me with many more blessings for which I am deeply thankful. For instance, to my surprise, I didn't feel alone or even lonely after David left to return to his family. Soon afterwards, I noticed an email from a friend I had printed out and left lying on a chair many months prior. It referred to a passage of Scripture in Hebrews 12 that speaks of the surrounding "cloud of witnesses," that is, those Christians who have gone to be with the Lord, yet still encourage us here on earth through their story of faith. I believe Babby is one of those witnesses. And most importantly, I realized then and now that the Lord is always with me and will never leave me.

22

A Gift from Babby

It was on a November morning in 2010, about fourteen months after Babby left this world, when the gift was found. It was a small, everyday item that I came across in the Sunday School classroom where Babby attended with me up until a couple months before he passed away. Maybe the gift was only a coincidence, but I believe it was a God-coincidence. On that Sunday, one of our class members was absent due to illness. It was typical for our class to send get-well cards with brief notes written by each of us to our fellow members who were in the hospital or sick at home. Since I was scheduled to be the Sunday School teacher that morning, I arrived at the room early and began scanning through the small inventory of cards we kept on a shelf to see what would be suitable to send. I picked up one card that was lying by itself. Opening it up, I saw the card was signed *"Babby"* in his handwriting. It was a sympathy card with no other name or handwriting on it.

"Good heavens!" I said under my breath, then stuck the card out of sight. I couldn't deal with that then. I had to get on with the task at hand and teach the lesson.

Emotionally, I was fighting the blues, dreading going home after church to a house bereft of family, except for my little dog, Chance. My son David and his family had left after celebrating Thanksgiving with me, and my other son Hollis had returned to his home too. The Thanksgiving-Christmas season accentuated my sense of loss and loneliness in general, and that Sunday in particular.

Yet God did not leave me dangling in the blues. Our pastor's sermon was about expectant hope, and that was just what I needed to hear. Also I enjoyed choir rehearsal Sunday afternoon as we practiced Christmas music. Singing joyful songs about Jesus and God's Word always lifts my spirits.

Clearly, God was ministering to me, but the best was yet to come.

After choir practice following the church service, I felt I had to show the card to someone or I was going to bust. Fortunately our music director, Ben, was still in the choir room, so I hurried back to the Sunday School room to find the card and show it to him. When I picked it up, I paused to read the message that was printed on the card, and I was deeply touched with the way it spoke to me.

"Look what I found in our Sunday School room," I said excitedly, trembling a little, showing Ben the card. On the inside of the card the words said:

> *May your heart be quieted*
> *by the gentle peace of God...*
> *strengthened by the*
> *promise of His care...*
> *and restful in the*
> *comfort of His Spirit.*

"In Sincere Sympathy," it concluded. Underneath that, Babby had written his name somewhat shakily, underlining it. I have no idea when or why he wrote his name on this card, as I told Ben. Printed inside the card was a Scripture passage that has been a comforting mainstay for me for years. I read the verse aloud to Ben, my voice filled with emotion: "Fear thou not, for I am with thee; be not dismayed; for I am thy God. I will strengthen thee; yea, I will help thee; yea I will uphold thee with the right hand of My righteousness."[1]

The significance of those words washed all over me. God had guided me to the card with Babby's handwriting in order to point me to God's promise. He promised not only to stay beside me on days when I felt the bleak loneliness of being without Babby after being married to him for fifty years, but God also promised to strengthen and hold me steady with His arm that never grows weak or tired. To me, that's what this card was saying. God knew how comforting that message would be for me, right at a time when I needed an extra comfort-gift that keeps on giving.

My husband's dementia was heartbreaking and difficult to deal with. I'll always be grateful for the many ways God and His people helped us get through those hard years and for the encouraging Scriptures and uplifting songs I sang with our church choir. The words and music drew me close to our Lord and helped me keep on trusting Him in my struggles with worry and fatigue.

I've missed Babby more than I can describe and life without him hasn't been easy, but the Lord has continued to comfort me. He reminds me every day that His love never fails and I feel the presence of His caring, guiding Holy Spirit.

I hope and pray that our story of God's faithfulness will encourage readers that He can help in their worst difficulties too, even in dementia.

> "Trust in the Lord with all your heart; do not depend on your own understanding. Seek His will in all you do, and He will show you which path to take."[2]

> "And when I was burdened with worries, you comforted me and made me feel secure."[3]

Thanks be to God!

Afterword
Written by David Hand

Dementia is hard. Caring for a loved one with dementia can be exhausting and incredibly challenging. But there is hope.

You've read my mother's story. She experienced hope and peace during the darkest days of caring for my dad, but it was only possible through her personal connection with Jesus Christ. It's my mom's desire that you would experience the same hope by beginning a personal, eternal relationship with Jesus. Here's how:

It is good news — fantastic news — that anyone can turn to God and be truly loved and accepted by Him. Through Jesus Christ's sacrificial death and resurrection, this is possible.

When Jesus began His ministry and started teaching the crowds, He told them that they must "repent and believe."[1]

His instructions to repent and believe still remain for us today. "But what exactly did Jesus mean by this?" you may ask. It means that Jesus is the Messiah and that by faith in Him alone, we will be saved. We must admit that we are sinners — even our best religious efforts are not enough to make our hearts clean from sin. We must believe that Jesus is the only Savior. Then we must consciously and willingly put our faith in Christ.

Putting our faith in Christ is a once-in-a-lifetime decision and the results are eternal. Repenting and believing means that Jesus' death and payment is applied to us. It means our sins are forgiven and removed "as far as the east is from the west"[2] forever.

The four principles of the *Would You Like to Know God Personally?*[3] visual presentation, created by Cru®, explain step by step what it means to repent and believe.

You can pray something like the following to ask Jesus to save you and begin an eternal relationship with Him. If you pray sincerely, whether you pray out loud or silently, the Lord will hear you:

> *Lord Jesus, I turn to you because I need you. I believe you are the Messiah. You are my only hope. My sin keeps me from you, but I come to you now just as I am, wanting to be forgiven and made new. Thank you for suffering and dying on the cross in my place. Please give me a new heart and mind. Take control of my life and help me to keep turning to you to follow you, moment by moment, for all my*

days on earth and in eternity. Thank you for loving me so much. I look forward to growing closer to you. Amen.

Here are four ways to continue to cultivate a growing relationship with Christ:

1. Find at least one or two Christians who truly love Jesus and tell them why you have turned to Jesus. Ask them if you can attend church with them. Intentionally seek people who will guide you in consistently following Jesus. Spend time talking with friends who love Jesus — learn from them and pray with them. Ask them to pray for you to grow closer to Jesus.
2. Read the Bible regularly. If you've never read it before and need help getting started, ask your friends to help. You can also turn to Bible.com or ask for a printed Bible from the church you attend. When you read the Bible, remember that it is, in fact, God's living word. Ask the Lord to open your mind and heart to hear what He says to you personally through the passages you read. Ask Him to change you through His Word. You don't have to start by reading large sections of the Bible all at once. Perhaps a good place to start is to read the section called John (the Gospel of

John.) Read one or two chapters at a time. Then discuss it with your friends who love Jesus.
3. Tell others about Jesus. In your own words, simply explain why you trusted in Jesus. Explain why it is significant for you personally that Jesus loves you.
4. Listen to what Jesus tells you to do and do it. You'll get to know Him much better as a loving Father as you obey Him in your thoughts, words, attitudes and actions. When you fail, honestly admit it to Him and move forward believing that He gives you strength and second chances.

APPENDIX
Written by David Hand

"Even to your old age and gray hairs I am he, I am he who will sustain you. I have made you and I will carry you; I will sustain you and I will rescue you."

Isaiah 46:4 NIV

If you are dealing with dementia as a caregiver or a patient, you may be pressed by a few challenging questions related to caring or suffering. My mother, the author of this book, has wrestled with several questions. Now, as I serve as caregiver for my mother, I'm doing some wrestling with questions too. Other caregivers of dementia patients have told us that it's normal to question the "whys," "hows," "how come...," and "what ifs" of dementia. It's also quite normal to become emotionally tired and stretched when you care for someone who has memory issues. Some of these hard questions have no complete answer, but I hope the following starting points will help.

Questions Related to Dementia:

1. Why does dementia exist?
2. What does God think about dementia?
3. Will God forsake people with dementia?
4. Why should people with dementia and their caregivers turn to God?
5. What if I forget about God?
6. What if my mind is gone and I can't remember enough to physically, socially or mentally thrive?
7. If I suspect I may have some form of dementia, what should I do to get help?

Hope for Weary Caregivers:

1. How do I care for myself as I care for my loved one who has dementia?
2. What does it look like to care well for my loved one who has dementia?
3. What if I feel reluctant to care for my loved one who has dementia?
4. Should I send my loved one who has dementia to a nursing home or memory care assisted living facility?

Questions Related to Dementia

1. Why does dementia exist?

Many people suffer terribly with Alzheimer's or another type of dementia. Currently there is no cure.

Dementia has caused so much pain and difficulty over the centuries that humanly speaking, we can't even measure it. It's impossible to answer the question of why. It is unfair to attempt a short, glib answer. A medical, technical or even a theological answer to this question leaves many unsatisfied. Yet the story of a man born blind whom Jesus healed, recorded in John 9:1-41, provides some profound and helpful perspective. In the endnotes section, you can read the entire story of the blind man[1] or see the link to a video of this passage courtesy of Jesus Film Project®.[2]

Dealing with dementia or any form of personal suffering can make us think that we have no ultimate hope in this life. Conversely, personal suffering can give us such a careful perspective on the fragility of life that we gain a new lens through which to view long-term hope via the immediate trials of suffering. It is the latter perspective that Jesus offers.

Medically speaking, there was no hope for the blind man.

Using his voice to call out and beg, the blind man made his presence known to people near the temple gate every day. Jesus saw him. The disciples heard him. Perhaps they had heard the man crying out several times prior to the moment when Jesus approached him.

It can be easy to tune out a beggar's voice, especially when you perceive that your priorities and business of the day are more important than the immediate needs of a man who must beg to find daily bread. Yet the disciples saw their Master decisively not tune out the blind man's voice. Jesus moved close to the man. Jesus wanted to give the man more than bread — He wanted him to have a brand new life.

Then the disciples asked Jesus, "Who sinned? This man or his parents, that he was born blind?"[3] Their question was based on the common belief of the day that physical disabilities or severe illnesses were a result of one's own evildoing. Beneath the surface, their "who" question hinted towards a paramount cornucopia of "why" questions they wanted their master to address:

Why did someone sin or do such terrible evil that this man had never seen anything but darkness for all the days of his life? Why do we have such evil in our hearts? Why does a good, merciful God punish people who do evil?

Why would God bring physical blindness on anyone? Why would God allow dementia to fall upon anyone's brain?

Jesus answered, "Neither this man nor his parents sinned, but this happened so that the works of God might be displayed in him."[4]

The Master said that the man was not born blind due to a punishment from God. Jesus healed the man to demonstrate the works of God, which are kindness and mercy towards people who live in a broken world — people constantly dealing with the effects of sin entering the world.

Dementia is not a punishment for sin. It is a result of sin entering the world. Sin causes spiritual blindness — a blindness to ourselves and a blindness towards God. When spiritually blind, we can not perceive our true condition as a sinful human in relation to a pure, holy, infinite God who alone lives in unapproachable light. Turning to God for healing and cleansing from sin — a healing which He invites everyone to experience — is our ultimate healing and gives us eternal, abundant life.

Healing from spiritual blindness is our ultimate good. And our ultimate need. That is why the story in John's gospel gives us such great hope that whether we have dementia or not, Jesus can give us a new life.

Just as some people find it difficult to talk about their loved one who struggles with dementia, many find it hard to admit their own spiritual condition — their spiritual blindness. Jesus is the only One who knows us and sees us as we are — spiritually blind, needy, filthy, sick. He is the only One who can forgive, cleanse and heal us of sin.

Even faithful believers and disciples of Jesus are not exempt from suffering — from God's "subjection of the creation to futility"[5] due to sin, as described in Paul's letter to the Romans. Disease and illness are part of the subjection to futility which every human encounters. However, believers are given a special promise for a time in the future when Jesus will remove all suffering from our presence and give us a new, redeemed, glorified body. A body and mind free from all shackles of dementia, forgetfulness or corruption. The constant comfort and teaching of the Holy Spirit provides such breaking and releasing of our chains that we long for the future day of our new bodies even more.

"And we believers also groan, even though we have the Holy Spirit within us as a foretaste of future glory, for we long for our bodies to be released from sin and suffering. We, too, wait with eager hope for the day when God will give us our full rights as his adopted children, including the new bodies he has promised us."[6]

"And we know that God causes everything to work together for the good of those who love God and are called according to his purpose for them."[7]

Some people who struggle with dementia for many years will find that their sense of connection with God becomes stronger and they become more confident in Jesus' love even during horrible suffering. Their life is very hard. Mentally and emotionally, they may seem like a wretched person. Yet they grow deeper and stronger in the currents of God's strong love for them.

The Bible gives much more attention to this topic. The story of Job, a man who lost all of his children and most of his vast wealth in one day, describes a personal journey of suffering. Job was afflicted with a terrible skin disease and suffered more than any man mentioned in the Bible other than Jesus. Yet he grew closer to God. Read the story of Job or listen to it via an audio Bible such as *her.BIBLE* to learn how Job responded to his sufferings.

Physical healing from dementia or any disability or disease is not the ultimate healing any of us can hope for. For those who put their trust and hope in the Savior Jesus, a guaranteed healing awaits in heaven while joyous hope, a brand new spiritual life and friendship with Him can be found in Christ moment by moment. This is good news.

2. What does God think about dementia?

Although my mother has written two dozen chapters sharing her story of how God greatly helped her deal with dementia as a caregiver, no one completely knows what God thinks about dementia. Just as there is no complete answer to "why does dementia exist," there are no intricate details which God has provided regarding His specific thoughts or actions concerning dementia. But generally speaking we do know how God views and responds to people with dementia.

God loves people. His love isn't subjective or theoretical. His love has an object — His people. By His nature and His acts, God constantly demonstrates His love towards humans. This is a fact. It is a premise on which all Christians base their beliefs. (See Romans 5:8 ESV and 1 John 4:10 NLT.)

The manner in which God loves people is extremely personal. He loves each person constantly, perfectly, in a personal way. In human terms, love is sometimes described as a two-way street. When we are loved, we reciprocate by loving the person who loves us. God wants to love and be known in a personal way. He wants a close, personal relationship with us.[8]

God by nature is all-knowing and ever present. This means He never forgets anything about Himself. He never forgets to love. He never fails to love fully or perfectly. The adjective used by several psalmists and prophets who wrote portions of the Old Testament to describe God's love is "steadfast."[9] His love is a never-ending, strong and personal show of mercy and grace towards us. God remembers His steadfast love towards us and He never forgets.

When we consider who God truly is, we realize that He is the only one from all time whose name and memory deserves to be remembered forever. (See Psalm 102:12 ESV.) Every human, no matter how relatively significant we are in comparison to other humans, falls short. However, incredibly, God stoops to draw near to us and show that He wants to remember us and love us.

I mentioned in the Foreword that my dad's life was changed noticeably when he experienced God in a personal way. The way my dad described it, he had never felt so loved. He was overpowered by the love of God. His spiritual blindness was taken away and he saw how much God loved him and how deeply he had been forgiven.

My father had always been a church attender and perhaps had a meaningful salvation experience early on in life. But during his mid-fifties when he saw how much God loved him, I began to notice many distinct changes in my dad's life. Several other people noticed as well.

I saw firsthand how he began to treat my mom with more kindness and humbly place her interests above his own. He had always cared for her. But after Dad experienced God's love in a personal way, he became more patient and kind. His language changed from self-absorbed and dishonoring God to edifying and God-honoring.

Into his middle and late fifties and sixties, God's steadfast love seemed to flow through my dad. He began to serve the Lord — in many ways totally behind the scenes. He volunteered at the state prison nearby — serving with Prison

Fellowship Ministries to lead Bible Studies for inmates. For several years he coordinated the Project Angel Tree program for Mitchell County — providing Christmas presents for the children of prison inmates who would not get to spend Christmas with their fathers.

The story of my dad's changed life is one among many stories of people who have experienced God's love and forgiveness. This shows me that the object of God's love is people — even people with dementia.

3. Will God forsake people with dementia?

The only people God forsakes are those who do evil by rejecting Him. Rejecting God is the ultimate evil. Anyone who sins rejects God. As humans, we all tend to reject God, even in subtle ways, by ignoring Him, circumnavigating Him or building our lives on the ultimate pursuit of our own image and desires rather than His.

So does God forsake every human? Fortunately, no. Just as He miraculously provided the blind man[10] with sight, God provides a way for anyone to have his or her infinite debt of sin erased. But God never forces Himself on anyone. He simply makes His love known in the most tangible and memorable way that could ever be possible —

by sending His one and only son Jesus to live and walk among us, living as human flesh and giving up His life as a sacrifice of love for us.

God extends a personal invitation for us to come to Him — to love, be loved and to find all that our soul needs in Him. We find much language of invitation in the Old and New Testaments through Jesus' very words. He invites us to come to Him much like we would invite dear friends to come join us for an exquisite dinner or special celebration. Here is just a small sampling of Scriptures where God gives us a personal invitation to come to Him:

"Is anyone thirsty? Come and drink — even if you have no money! Come, take your choice of wine or milk — it's all free! Why spend your money on food that does not give you strength? Why pay for food that does you no good? Listen to me, and you will eat what is good. You will enjoy the finest food. Come to me with your ears wide open. Listen, and you will find life. I will make an everlasting covenant with you. I will give you all the unfailing love I promised to David."[11]

"Now on the last day, the great [day] of the feast, Jesus stood and cried out, saying, 'If anyone is thirsty, let him come to Me and drink. The one who believes in Me, as the Scripture said, From his innermost being will flow rivers of living water.'"[12]

"The Spirit and the bride say, 'Come.' Let anyone who hears this say, 'Come.' Let anyone who is thirsty come. Let anyone who desires drink freely from the water of life."[13]

"Come to me, all of you who are weary and carry heavy burdens, and I will give you rest."[14]

Not only does God invite us to come to Him, but God also pursues people He loves. He is relentless to demonstrate His kindness and love towards people — even unworthy sinners whom He doesn't despise, but treasures!

We find many instances in Scripture where Jesus could have rejected or forsaken people who seemed quite unworthy of love or His invitation to come. Yet in those instances, Jesus went out of His way to pursue and invite the wayward person to come near to Him. We see the example of the corrupt tax collector Zacchaeus, where Jesus not only stopped to have an intentional conversation with him, He said, "I must come to your house and dine with you today."[15] So Jesus went as far as to invite Himself over to this disreputable sinner's house to enjoy food and company with him. Another time, Jesus went out of His way to meet an unpopular woman who had had several failed marriages. He chose to disclose to her — prior to announcing it to the more reputable people in her town — that He was the awaited Messiah. He offered her constant "living water" for her soul.[16] You may view this passage of Scripture via a Jesus Film Project™ video.[17]

Even during the excruciating moments while Jesus hung on the cross during crucifixion, Jesus was intentional about finding and pursuing people who otherwise would have been forsaken. A few feet away, a condemned criminal hung on another cross and called out to Jesus, "Remember me when you come into your Kingdom."[18] Jesus responded clearly to the criminal that because he had faith in Jesus, he would receive eternal love and eternal life. "Today you will be with me in paradise,"[19] the Lord said.

People who accept His invitation to "come to Me" will indeed live with Him forever. It doesn't matter if we seem worthy or not. The fact is, we're not worthy. No one is worthy of His invitation. Yet whether we have dementia or any type of dysfunction, we can be sure that He pursues us and humbly invites us to come.

4. Why should people with dementia and their caregivers turn to God?

Sin is far worse than dementia. Jesus is the only answer for the penalty and self-corruption of sin. He willingly gave Himself to be crucified as a sacrificial payment for our sins — including past, present and future sins. He knew that we had no ability to overcome our sin and no means to pay for it. He died in our place because He loves us.

A major theme of this book is hope. My mother wrote about her journey with my father's dementia to show that there is hope in suffering, but eternal hope can only become a reality through knowing Christ. My mother has turned to Christ and has been walking in the eternal hope of Jesus for quite some time. As I wrote above in the answer to "What does God think about dementia," my father turned to Christ and experienced His deep love for many years before his passing. Yet my dad was a sinner and my mom is a sinner. As anyone who has parents should attest, it is impossible for parents to hide their sinfulness from their children. And likewise it's impossible for children to veil their sinfulness from their parents! Sin cannot be overcome on our own. We all need a Savior.

The following psalm was written several hundred years before Jesus was born, yet it speaks of the extreme goodness of God and His rescue of sinners through Jesus. The psalmist gives an answer to those who seek a long, fulfilling life (see verse 12):

> "Taste and see that the LORD is good. Oh, the joys of those who take refuge in him! 9 Fear

the LORD, you his godly people, for those who fear him will have all they need. 10 Even strong young lions sometimes go hungry, but those who trust in the LORD will lack no good thing. 11 Come, my children, and listen to me, and I will teach you to fear the LORD. 12 Does anyone want to live a life that is long and prosperous? 13 Then keep your tongue from speaking evil and your lips from telling lies! 14 Turn away from evil and do good. Search for peace, and work to maintain it. 15 The eyes of the LORD watch over those who do right; his ears are open to their cries for help. 16 But the LORD turns his face against those who do evil; he will erase their memory from the earth. 17 The LORD hears his people when they call to him for help. He rescues them from all their troubles. 18 The LORD is close to the brokenhearted; he rescues those whose spirits are crushed."[20]

Consider the significance of verse 16: "But the LORD turns his face against those who do evil; he will erase their memory from the earth."

Sin is rejecting — an intentional forgetting of God. We choose to do what may seem relatively good or "better than other people," but anytime we reject God it is only evil at the end of the day.

Although sin is an intentional rejection of God, it can also be subtle and deceptive. Sin can seem good or true on the outside, but the core is rotten. Just like dementia brings corruption and chaos to thoughts and memories, sin brings corruption to our entire being.

God is holy. We are not. He is supreme and paramount in everything He does. The offense of our sin is so great and the rottenness of it is so deep that He must completely cut off — like an amputation of a grossly infected limb — even the memory of those who reject the Lord.

Jesus paid the ultimate sacrifice for us. The payment was completed on the cross when Jesus died. But then Jesus rose from the grave. His sacrifice was activated and validated by His resurrection.

Even though Jesus' sacrifice is complete and is available once for all time, we must individually turn to Him to accept His sacrifice on our behalf. His offer of complete forgiveness and total healing stands available for everyone. But we receive His offer only when we repent and turn to Him in belief.

5. What if I forget about God? How do I turn back to Him?

God first loved us. Our initial love for Him and our initial turning to Him was out of response to His love. Our final act of love for Him as believers will also be a response to His love. Turning back to Him is always a response to His initiative of love.

Forgetting about God can mean that we intentionally choose to ignore Him. This is akin to rejecting God — which I described in the response to question #4 above. Over a period of time, if we grow accustomed to ignoring God frequently, our thoughts and conscience can become conditioned to filter out His attempts to love us and communicate with us. Spiritual blindness clouds us again. God does not forget about us or sever His relationship with us, but we may feel estranged from Him.

All who walk as a Christian have seasons, however lengthy or brief, of when we forget about God. Essentially, any time we sin as we walk with God, we have replaced Him or forgotten about Him in exchange for something much less than God — something that we crave for our own little self glory rather than God's glory.

The apostle Paul described it this way, "I don't really understand myself, for I want to do what is right, but I don't do it. Instead, I do what I hate."[21]

If He brings even the smallest measure of His kindness and love to our mind, we can turn back to Him. This is because His kindness always leads us to repentance.

Whether or not we have dementia, continuing to walk in closeness and fellowship with God is dependent on His unmerited kindness, not on our mental abilities. Even if dementia robs our minds of the ability to remember what is written in the Bible, for example, or details of God's character, He will always be faithful to show us kindness. No matter how much our own memories fade, His love never fails. He will always tap us on the shoulder in some way — with some personal reminder that says, "This is Me. I am here. I love you" — to lift the fog of forgetfulness, confusion or even distracted wandering.

These personal reminders from God can come in many various forms: Words spoken to us by people; a simple hug; a song; memories that pop into our head, including memories of God's Word; a beautiful sunrise; visiting a scenic place; feeling God's presence; recalling times in the past when we received tangible generosity that only God could have provided; the taste of a home-cooked specialty; the aroma of your favorite perfume or even the greeting of your dog when you come in the door.

God provides the personal reminder and the solution to turn back to Him. God calls the solution repentance. To repent is to change your mind for the better. That is constantly what we should be doing throughout each day.

When we forget about God, it's important to remember that our relationship with God is never severed, but our fellowship with Him often needs restoring and refreshing.

Repentance is a repeated act that restores fellowship with Christ. Christians all over the world have experienced tremendous times of revival and closeness with God when they practiced regular repentance.

The visual presentation called *Satisfied?*[22] explains the simple process of turning back to God, repenting and living completely and joyfully by faith. All of this is described as spiritual breathing — both exhaling and inhaling. We exhale by turning away from our forgetting God. Then inhale by turning towards God by faith, putting our faith in His work to restore and forgive us. As often as we are aware of sin in our life, we can breathe spiritually.[23] Walking and breathing with God in this way allows His presence to remain fresh. My life has never been the same since I started to practice spiritual breathing.

6. What if my mind is totally gone and I can't remember enough to physically, socially and mentally thrive?

No one wants to experience the advanced stages of dementia. Because we are designed for connection and relationship, we all want to live in close mental and relational harmony with our loved ones up until the very end. But it is possible for dementia patients that a day will come, as it did for my dad, when the grip of dementia overcomes the capability to thrive — even the ability to have a relational connection with loved ones. Not all dementia patients will experience a total inability to thrive mentally, socially and physically, but some will. Nevertheless, not even this will separate us from the love of Christ and His promises.

> "Who shall separate us from the love of Christ? Shall tribulation, or distress, or persecution, or famine, or nakedness, or peril, or sword?"[24]

> "Even to your old age and gray hairs I am he, I am he who will sustain you. I have made you and I will carry you; I will sustain you and I will rescue you."[25]

> "Jesus Christ is the same yesterday and today and forever."[26]

God never changes. He loved us in the past, He loves us today and for those who are saved, He will love us through all eternity.

One of the names of God is Jehovah Rapha: The LORD who heals. It is part of who God is to heal people now and at the end of time.[27]

We know that healing from dementia is not the ultimate healing any of us can hope for. Healing from spiritual death is. Nevertheless, our physical well being is influenced by and, in one sense, contained inside of our spiritual healing. In other words, our eternal spiritual life envelops our finite, physical life.

Christ superintends the process of healing and redemption in our lives. It is a process that we participate in, by faith, as we walk with Him. It continues all the days of our earthly life. But our healing is completed in full when we die, leave our earthly life and fully enter into His presence.

One who can't remember his son's name or even his own name here on earth will remember and thrive in heaven. His corrupted memories and mental capacities will be transformed to yield uninhibited closeness in relationship. Perfect harmony. Constant thriving in relationship with God and others.

The spiritual process of walking with God is not dependent on our ability to thrive on earth. The Superintendent of our healing will sovereignly lead us through whatever depths of dementia are meant to be in our journey. His power is made perfect in our weakness.[28] Every part of us becomes perfected and whole in His eternal glory.

7. If I suspect that I may have some form of dementia, what should I do first to get help?

Pray. Ask God for specific wisdom. Ask Him to help you see what to do and the strength to carry out the first steps of what you can do. There may be immediate needs you have — physical and tangible — which God can provide. Also take a moment to ask God for the intangible and spiritual things which you deeply need as well. Things such as supernatural peace, a willingness and ability to listen to God, patience to wait or endure the unknowns of the future and an intuitive understanding for your friends to best know how to come alongside you. Only God can provide these things.

You could pray something like the following:

Lord Jesus, I need help. You are present here with me and You are listening and caring. I want to trust You with the unknowns about my mental and physical condition, now and into the future. Please give me Your peace. Please guide me with wisdom and through the care and guidance of other people whom you will put in my path. Most of all, help my mind and heart to be joyfully content in knowing You — even through dementia. I trust you and love you Lord.

Contact your doctor. It's good to ask someone — a family member or trusted friend — to go with you to your doctor's appointment. Your doctor can conduct some simple, painless tests to determine how much cognitive dysfunction or memory loss that you are experiencing.

Make a list of people and resources you have today — anyone or anything you feel could help you on your journey. Continue to expand this list as God provides. You can use it as an encouragement to see all of the things you can be thankful for — people and things which can make your dementia journey easier.

Hope for Weary Caregivers

1. How do I care for myself as I care for my loved one who has dementia?

"How do I get off of this discouraging, draining ride?" I remember thinking. Trying to ensure my dad's good care and safety as well as forecast what the days ahead might hold for a dementia patient felt like a combination of a whack-a-mole game and slogging through cold mud. As I came alongside my parents when Mom served as Dad's primary caregiver in his last days, I remember feeling drastically unprepared for each day. Sometimes there was a need that had to be met for my parents that I either did not know how to meet or just had very limited capacity to meet. I felt a deep sense of inadequacy. Even today as I now care for my mom, I am in over my head. It's not just a feeling, it's a constant reality.

Truly, the caregiver needs as much care and help, in a different form, as the dementia patient.

To begin to gain relief and feel hope for ourselves as caregivers, we must first have the perspective that it is ok to care for ourselves. We must take time to receive care from others and care for ourselves when we are serving a loved one with dementia. Making time to care for ourselves can be challenging — especially for caregivers with a high sense of responsibility. But we can implement self-care as a regular practice. Over time, the results of this practice can be positively crucial.

Part of the practice of self-care involves the challenging, firm action of saying "no" to serving your loved one on certain days or certain hours so that you can get some rest. Another part of this practice may involve asking others for help far more often than is comfortable for you. I remember feeling uncomfortable even when I asked several people to pray for me. But having others pray for me was an enormous help.

Jesus said, "Come to me, all of you who are weary and carry heavy burdens, and I will give you rest."[29] Our emotions and bodies are quickly depleted as caregivers. In Jesus, we find an unending source of rest. It is critical that we frequently turn to Jesus and ask Him for help and for rest. Finding time and space to talk with Him alone and listen to His Word is a balm to the soul. Jesus meets us where we are emotionally. He is able to sympathize with our overwhelming weakness.[30]

2. What does it look like to care well for my loved one who has dementia?

Caring well requires love. This type of love is a selfless love. Jesus is the source of selfless love. Being loved by and cared for by Jesus gives us more than enough empathizing love to put others' interests above our own. Caring well looks like a person who simply depends on Christ for everything. Only when He loves people through us can we care well.

Caring well for another person also means caring well for yourself. If dementia caregiving could be compared to an in-flight emergency during an airline flight, we must first strap on our own oxygen mask before giving oxygen to our loved one. Maintaining our own health and well being as caregivers is like essential oxygen. Our ongoing, personal walk with God gives us well-being — even during challenging times.

There are several support groups and online discussion groups where you can learn a lot from other caregivers. To see if there are Alzheimer's support groups in your area, go to Alz.org. We have even turned to YouTube® to learn from other experienced caregivers. Some of the videos we found helpful are found on the "Dementia with Grace" YouTube channel[32]: @DementiaWithGrace. There are several other social media channels regarding caregiving or dementia which you may find helpful. Simply search for "dementia caregivers" on YouTube or elsewhere.

3. What if I feel reluctant to care for my loved one who has dementia?

Reluctance is a negative feeling that leads to one displaying actions or inclinations of hesitancy, aversion or unwillingness.[31] Feeling reluctant can be a natural reaction when faced with becoming the primary caregiver for a dementia patient. I admit I have struggled with this feeling. While the feeling can be a natural and immediate reaction, when left unchecked, reluctance can lead to actions that are not good. Running away, distancing yourself or ignoring your loved one with dementia are all examples of inappropriate actions to avoid.

You may have a loved one recently diagnosed with dementia and now you're faced with a decision of when and how to be involved to help. Obviously this can feel very heavy. But you are never alone.

Since God is omnipresent and always listening, we can ask Him for supernatural help as frequently as we want and it never frustrates Him. In fact, it pleases Him when we ask Him for good things. Also, it's ok to ask other people repeatedly for help. But it's not ok simply to turn your back and walk away from your parents or loved ones who have no one else to help them.

No caregiver does it perfectly. Even the best caregivers feel like walking away sometimes. Sometimes we wrongly assume that other people will step in and take responsibility to provide care without us asking. Or we tend not to ask others for as much help as we need. We tend to look at the mountain of needs in caregiving and become overwhelmed and afraid.

Instead of walking away in fear, the Lord invites us to toss our fears onto His back. Even when we fail in caregiving, Jesus uses our experience to help us depend on Him even more. He never fails. He has limitless love and resources. He never leaves or forsakes those He loves.

4. Should I send my loved one who has dementia to a nursing home or memory care assisted living facility?

My mom had made plans, although only contingency plans, to move Dad into a nursing home if it became necessary. She wanted him to live at home, but knew that his condition might worsen to the point where it would actually be detrimental for him to stay in his own house.

Several nursing homes or assisted living facilities offer specialized memory care units — with dedicated staff experienced in serving Alzheimers or other dementia patients. With around-the-clock professional nurses and aides on site and clean, private rooms, these facilities can be a safe and helpful place for our loved ones. However, especially if your loved one's mind isn't fully capable of making decisions regarding his or her own care, the choice and details surrounding a move to a memory care facility can be stressful or overwhelming.

"Am I just giving up on him if I send him to a nursing home?" The question loomed and became more and more of an accusative thought as my dad's dementia journey dragged on. Later I realized that there is a huge difference between giving up and asking for help. Moving your loved one into a care facility is not giving up responsibility, it is actually a sharing of that responsibility. Any care facility worth its salt will allow and even encourage you as a loved one to continue to be very involved in providing emotional support and care. Maintaining a daily connection when your loved one lives away from you in a care facility can help tremendously.

Some dementia patients seem to do better and maintain more cognitive function when they remain at home or in a very stable, familiar environment. Seeking professional services to assist you in your home may be an option. If so, this may feel more complicated at first but depending on your situation, could be most helpful to you as a caregiver and provide a high level of care for your loved one. Even if you aren't able to hire professional services, but other family members or loved ones can physically assist with regular duties at your home, this could end up being a better option in your situation.

The bottom line is that there is no "one-size-fits-all" answer. No formula. The best results for your loved one in terms of where to care for him or her may vary over time. It takes discernment and sacrificial empathizing to see what would work best for you and your loved one.

Prayer and guidance from the Lord can superintend the decision of when or if to move towards full-time professional care. Your doctor will need to be involved in the decision and can provide resources for the transition, if a move becomes necessary.

Endnotes

Chapter 2

1. John 14:27 NIV
2. Gaither, Bill and Gloria. "Because He Lives." United Methodist Hymnal 1989, Church Hymnal, p. 364. copyright 1971 William J. Gaither. https://hymnary.org/text/god_sent_his_son_they_called_him_jesus
3. Psalm 98:4 KJV

Chapter 3

1. Joncas, Micheal. "On Eagle's Wings." United Methodist Hymnal Music Supplement II 1993, Church Hymnal, p. 143. copyright 1979 New Dawn Music. https://hymnary.org/text/you_who_dwell_in_the_shelter_joncas
2. Psalm 91:1-2 NLT
3. Martin, Civilla D. "His Eye is on the Sparrow," 1905, public domain. https://hymnary.org/text/why_should_i_feel_discouraged
4. Brewer, Jehoiadia. "The Hiding Place," 1793, public domain. https://hymnary.org/text/hail_sovereign_love_that_first_began
5. Isaiah 12:2 NLT

Chapter 4

1. Isaiah 41:10 NLT

2. Everest, Charles W. "Take up Thy Cross," 1883, public domain. https://hymnary.org/text/take_up_thy_cross_the_savior_said_if_tho
3. Rowe, James. "Love Lifted Me," 1912, public domain. https://hymnary.org/text/i_was_sinking_deep_in_sin_far_from_the

Chapter 6

1. Isaiah 43:2,4,5 NLT
2. 1 Corinthians 13:7,13 NLT
3. 2 Corinthians 2:19 NLT
4. Lemmel, Helen H. "Turn Your Eyes Upon Jesus," 1922, public domain. https://hymnary.org/text/o_soul_are_you_weary_and_troubled
5. Ibid.

Chapter 8

1. Psalm 23:4 NKJV

Chapter 9

1. Hebrews 13:5 NLT
2. Psalms 23:4 NLT
3. Romans 8:37 NLT
4. 2 Corinthians 12:9 NLT
5. Matthew 6:34 ESV
6. Matthew 6:34 The Message
7. ten Boom, Corrie, et al. The Hiding Place. United States, Baker Publishing Group, 2006. page 29. https://www.google.com/books/edition/_/RfSsXCi9FxoC?sa=X&ved=2ahUKEwjMwaPq_4n2AhVvTTABHXUJDkEQ8fIDegQIKhBx

8. Firth, Jim "I Have a Hope," 1992, https://www.justsomelyrics.com/263661/rick-muchow-i-have-a-hope-lyrics.html

Chapter 10
1. John 14:27 NLT
2. Isaiah 41:10 NLT
3. 2 Corinthians 12:9 NIV
4. Philippians 4:13 NKJV

Chapter 13
1. 2 Corinthians 12:9 ESV

Chapter 14
1. Psalm 46:10 ESV
2. John 14:27 ESV Note: "I personalized this verse for myself by adding my name after Jesus states that He gives peace to all of you."
3. Reference to Isaiah 43:2 ESV
4. Reference to Isaiah 46:4 NIV
5. Reference to Isaiah 41:10 NLT Note: I personalized this verse for myself, as indicated by the (parenthesis marks), in my prayer journal.
6. Reference to Romans 8:28 NIV
7. Reference to Isaiah 66:13 NIV
8. Reference to Hebrews 13:5 ESV
9. Reference to Proverbs 3:5-6 NKJV Note: I personalized this verse for myself, as indicated by the (parenthesis marks), in my prayer journal.
10. Reference to 2 Corinthians 12:9 NASB
11. Reference to 1 Peter 5:7 NASB

12. Reference to Matthew 28:20 NLT
13. Reference to Deuteronomy 33:27 ESV
14. Reference to Isaiah 40:30-31 AMP
15. Scriven, Joseph Medlicott. "What a Friend We Have in Jesus," 1855; public domain. https://hymnary.org/text/what_a_friend_we_have_in_jesus_all_our_s
16. Psalm 23:1 ESV
17. Psalm 23:2-3 KJV

Chapter 15

1. Browning, Elizabeth Barrett. "How Do I Love Thee? (Sonnet 43)." Sonnets from the Portuguese, London: Caradoc Press, 1906. Public domain.
2. 1 Corinthians 13:7-8 NKJV
3. Reference to Deuteronomy 33:27 ESV

Chapter 16

1. Psalm 23:1 ESV
2. Psalm 23:2-3 KJV
3. Reference to Psalm 46:10 ESV
4. Psalm 23:4 KJV
5. Psalm 23:5 ESV
6. Psalm 23:6 NLT

Chapter 17

1. Mark 4:39 ESV
2. Psalm 46:10 ESV
3. 1 Thessalonians 5:18 ESV
4. Reference to Philippians 2:13 Amplified Version, 2015

Chapter 20

1. "When the Saints Go Marching In," Negro Spiritual, public domain. https://hymnary.org/text/o_when_the_saints_go_marching_in

Chapter 21

1. Isaiah 54:4a,5,10 NIV

Chapter 22

1. Isaiah 41:10 KJV
2. Proverbs 3:5-6 NLT
3. Psalm 94:19 CEV

Afterword

1. Reference to Mark 1:15 ESV
2. Reference to Psalm 103:12 NIV
3. View the visual presentation — <u>Would you like to know God personally</u>? by Cru® here: https://godtoolsapp.com/en/tools/know-god-personally/demo/

Appendix

1. Read the entire story of the blind man below at the end of this section. The entire contents of John 9 NLT are included.
2. Watch a video of the story of the blind man as recorded in John 9 here, courtesy of Jesus Film Project®: https://www.jesusfilm.org/watch/life-of-jesus-gospel-of-john.html/blind-man-healed/english.html
3. John 9:2 ESV

4. John 9:3 NIV
5. Reference to Romans 8:20 NKJV
6. Romans 8:20 NLT
7. Romans 8:28 NLT
8. See Isaiah 43:1 NLT to read how God has gone to great lengths to have a close, personal relationship with us.
9. Reference to Psalm 63:3 ESV and dozens of other verses in the Old Testament where the writer specifically describes God's love as "steadfast love."
10. Read the entire story of the blind man below at the end of this section. The entire contents of John 9 NLT are included.
11. Isaiah 55:1-3 NLT
12. John 7:37-38 NASB20
13. Revelation 22:17 NLT
14. Matthew 11:28 NLT
15. Reference to Luke 19:5 ESV
16. Reference to John 4:10-14 ESV
17. View this passage via a Jesus Film Project™ video: https://www.jesusfilm.org/watch/magdalena.html/magdalena-the-woman-at-the-well/english.html
18. Luke 23:42 NLT
19. Reference to Luke 23:43 NLT
20. Psalm 34:8-18 NLT
21. Romans 7:15 NLT
22. View the visual presentation — Satisfied? by Cru® here: https://knowgod.com/en/satisfied
23. Note: The term "spiritual breathing" does not appear in the Bible. This is only an illustrative term used to explain the Biblical process of

regular repentance and living by faith in the midst of our own brokenness. This is a vital practice for all Christians. It is explained well in the booklet created by Cru® — <u>Satisfied?</u> https://knowgod.com/en/satisfied

24. Romans 8:35 NKJV
25. Isaiah 46:4 NIV
26. Hebrews 13:8 ESV
27. Reference to Exodus 15:26 NLT and Isaiah 61:1-3 NLT
28. Reference to 2 Corinthians 12:9 ESV
29. Matthew 11:28 NLT
30. Reference to Hebrews 4:15-16 ESV
31. Definition of reluctant https://www.merriam-webster.com/dictionary/reluctant
32. www.youtube.com/@DementiaWithGrace

The Story of the Man Born Blind
(John 9:1-41 NLT)

1 As Jesus was walking along, he saw a man who had been blind from birth. 2 "Rabbi," his disciples asked him, "why was this man born blind? Was it because of his own sins or his parents' sins?" 3 "It was not because of his sins or his parents' sins," Jesus answered. "This happened so the power of God could be seen in him. 4 We must quickly carry out the tasks assigned us by the one who sent us. The night is coming, and then no one can work. 5 But while I am here in the world, I am the light of the world."

6 Then he spit on the ground, made mud with the saliva, and spread the mud over the blind man's eyes. 7 He told him, "Go wash yourself in the pool of Siloam" (Siloam means "sent"). So the man went and washed and came back seeing!

8 His neighbors and others who knew him as a blind beggar asked each other, "Isn't this the man who used to sit and beg?" 9 Some said he was, and

others said, "No, he just looks like him!" But the beggar kept saying, "Yes, I am the same one!" 10 They asked, "Who healed you? What happened?" 11 He told them, "The man they call Jesus made mud and spread it over my eyes and told me, 'Go to the pool of Siloam and wash yourself.' So I went and washed, and now I can see!" 12 "Where is he now?" they asked. "I don't know," he replied.

13 Then they took the man who had been blind to the Pharisees, 14 because it was on the Sabbath that Jesus had made the mud and healed him. 15 The Pharisees asked the man all about it. So he told them, "He put the mud over my eyes, and when I washed it away, I could see!" 16 Some of the Pharisees said, "This man Jesus is not from God, for he is working on the Sabbath." Others said, "But how could an ordinary sinner do such miraculous signs?" So there was a deep division of opinion among them.

17 Then the Pharisees again questioned the man who had been blind and demanded, "What's your opinion about this man who healed you?" The man replied, "I think he must be a prophet." 18 The Jewish leaders still refused to believe the man had been blind and could now see, so they called in his parents. 19 They asked them, "Is this your son? Was he born blind? If so, how can he now see?" 20 His

parents replied, "We know this is our son and that he was born blind, 21 but we don't know how he can see or who healed him. Ask him. He is old enough to speak for himself." 22 His parents said this because they were afraid of the Jewish leaders, who had announced that anyone saying Jesus was the Messiah would be expelled from the synagogue. 23 That's why they said, "He is old enough. Ask him."

24 So for the second time they called in the man who had been blind and told him, "God should get the glory for this, because we know this man Jesus is a sinner." 25 "I don't know whether he is a sinner," the man replied. "But I know this: I was blind, and now I can see!"

26 "But what did he do?" they asked. "How did he heal you?" 27 "Look!" the man exclaimed. "I told you once. Didn't you listen? Why do you want to hear it again? Do you want to become his disciples, too?" 28 Then they cursed him and said, "You are his disciple, but we are disciples of Moses! 29 We know God spoke to Moses, but we don't even know where this man comes from." 30 "Why, that's very strange!" the man replied. "He healed my eyes, and yet you don't know where he comes from? 31 We know that God doesn't listen to sinners, but he is ready to hear those who worship him and do his will. 32 Ever since the world began, no one has been

able to open the eyes of someone born blind. 33 If this man were not from God, he couldn't have done it." 34 "You were born a total sinner!" they answered. "Are you trying to teach us?" And they threw him out of the synagogue.

35 When Jesus heard what had happened, he found the man and asked, "Do you believe in the Son of Man?" 36 The man answered, "Who is he, sir? I want to believe in him." 37 "You have seen him," Jesus said, "and he is speaking to you!" 38 "Yes, Lord, I believe!" the man said. And he worshiped Jesus. 39 Then Jesus told him, "I entered this world to render judgment — to give sight to the blind and to show those who think they see that they are blind." 40 Some Pharisees who were standing nearby heard him and asked, "Are you saying we're blind?" 41 "If you were blind, you wouldn't be guilty," Jesus replied. "But you remain guilty because you claim you can see."

Made in the USA
Columbia, SC
31 March 2023